THE ESTABLISHMENT
OF THE EUROPEAN
HEGEMONY

1415-1715

the text of this book is printed
on 100% recycled paper

THE ESTABLISHMENT OF THE EUROPEAN HEGEMONY 1415-1715

Trade and Exploration in the Age of the Renaissance

Third Edition, Revised

J. H. PARRY

HARPER TORCHBOOKS
Harper & Row, Publishers
New York, Hagerstown, San Francisco, London

79 80   20 19 18 17 16 15 14

CONTENTS

INTRODUCTION: THE BOUNDS OF CHRISTENDOM, 1415   7

1   THE TOOLS OF THE EXPLORERS
     (i) Charts   13
     (ii) Ships   19
     (iii) Guns   24

2   'CHRISTIANS AND SPICES'
     (i) The sea crusaders   26
     (ii) The Cape of Storms   29
     (iii) The spice trade   32
     (iv) The Portuguese Indies   35

3   THE NEW WORLD
     (i) The Fortunate Isles   39
     (ii) Discovery   42
     (iii) The interpretation of discovery   45
     (iv) The division of the world   49

4   THE SILVER EMPIRE
     (i) The Spanish conquest   54
     (ii) The theory of empire   57
     (iii) Soldiers, missionaries and lawyers   60
     (iv) Atlantic trade and the silver fleets   64

5   FISHERMEN, EXPLORERS AND SLAVERS
     (i) The Atlantic fisheries   68
     (ii) The search for a northern passage   70
     (iii) The interlopers in America   73
     (iv) The privateers   76

6 THE STRUGGLE FOR EASTERN TRADE
- (i) The Muslim East — 80
- (ii) The decline of Portuguese power — 83
- (iii) The Companies — 86
- (iv) The Dutch East Indies — 90

7 THE ENGLISH PLANTATIONS
- (i) The theory of settlement — 93
- (ii) The planting Companies — 91
- (iii) The Puritans — 107

8 RIVAL EMPIRES IN AMERICA
- (i) The French in Canada — 107
- (ii) West Indian rivalries — 110
- (iii) The Portuguese in Brazil — 114
- (iv) The Dutch on the high seas — 116

9 THE OLD COLONIAL SYSTEM
- (i) The plantations in 1660 — 120
- (ii) The Acts of Trade — 123
- (iii) New York and New England — 126
- (iv) Louisiana and Hudson's Bay — 130

10 TRADE AND DOMINION IN THE EAST
- (i) Exploration and expansion in the Far East — 134
- (ii) Dutch rule in the islands — 139
- (iii) Rival powers in India — 143

11 SLAVERY AND THE WAR FOR TRADE
- (i) Slavery in Spanish America — 149
- (ii) Slavery in the Sugar Islands — 152
- (iii) The *Asientos* — 155
- (iv) The Spanish succession — 158

12 EPILOGUE: THE BOUNDS OF CHRISTENDOM, 1715 — 162

Suggestions for further reading — 170

Index — 173

INTRODUCTION: THE BOUNDS OF

CHRISTENDOM, 1415

One of the most striking features of the history of the last two hundred years has been the dominant influence exerted by Europeans outside Europe. The 'expansion of Europe' was not, of course, deliberately planned, nor was it willingly accepted by non-Europeans, but in the eighteenth and nineteenth centuries it proved irresistible; so much so, that the western nations devoted much of their energy to quarrelling over the spoils. The foundations of European dominance were prepared in the fifteenth century and firmly laid in the sixteenth and seventeenth. In those centuries sea-faring Europeans visited almost every part of the world. They met and conquered a great variety of primitive races. They met also many peoples to whom they were themselves barbarians, peoples who were wealthier, more numerous, and to all appearance more powerful than the western invaders. None of these peoples escaped European influence, whether social, religious, commercial or technical. Many of them fell under European rule; and at the same time many of the world's empty spaces were filled by people of European extraction. What were the motives which impelled European nations, from the fifteenth century onward, to embark on a career of overseas expansion? What were the social and technical abilities which gave that expansion such startling success?

In many directions the fifteenth century was for Western Europe a period of contraction, not of expansion. The Chinese Empire was by far the most powerful and most civilised State in the world at that time. It had been governed, at the height of Europe's Middle Age, by a Tartar dynasty whose dominions had included not only China

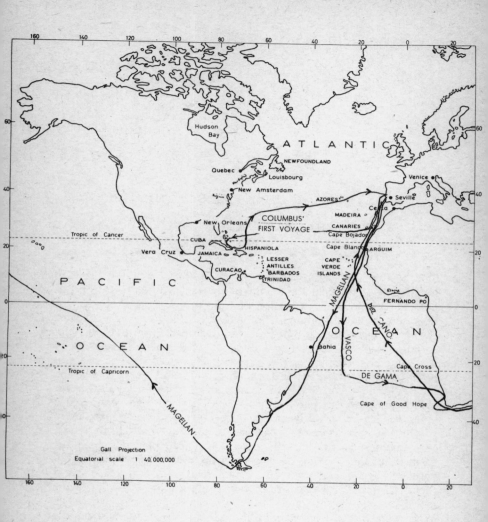

| | | | | | | | | | | |
|40|60|80|100|120|140|160|180| | | |

Archangel

PACIFIC

HORMUZ   Tropic of Cancer

Mecca   Diu   Surat   Calcutta   Canton

           Goa   Bombay   MAGELLAN

Aden   SOCOTRA   Masulipatam   OCEAN

        Calicut   Madras

           CEYLON Pondicherry   DEL CANO

                      Malacca   TERNATE   TIDORE

VASCO DE GAMA   AMBOINA

           Batavia Macassar   BANDA ISLANDS

        Sunda Strait

INDIAN

OCEAN   Tropic of Capricorn

           DEL CANO

Cape Agulhas

        Gall Projection
        Equatorial scale   1 : 40,000,000   TASMANIA

| | | | | | | | | |
|40|60|80|100|120|140|160|180|

proper, but Mongolia, Turkestan and part of Russia. This Tartar
dynasty at one time had shown toleration, even friendliness, towards
Christianity. Europeans had visited its Court and Franciscan missionaries had preached within its dominions; but the moment of
Christian opportunity had passed in the middle of the fourteenth
century, when the rule of the Tartar Khans had been overthrown by
a native dynasty, the Mings. Two other great religions, Buddhism
and Islam, divided Central Asia between them to the exclusion of
Christianity, and communication between Far East and Far West
had ceased. South of China, the kingdoms of Indo-China and the
East Indian islands, Hindu in origin, by the fifteenth century
were falling rapidly under the influence of Islam. In India, civilised
and powerful Hindu states were increasingly threatened by Muslim
pressure. Nearer to Europe, the Muslim communities of the Near
East were falling more and more under the military leadership of
the Ottoman Turks, fanatical semi-nomad warriors who were about
to engulf the remnants of the Byzantine Empire and to dominate
the whole eastern Mediterranean. They took Constantinople in
1453; early in the following century they were to conquer Egypt
and Syria, and having overrun the Balkans, were to press along the
Danube towards the heart of Central Europe. Islam, and not
European Christendom, was the most obviously expanding community in the fifteenth century.

Military and religious rivalry between Christendom and Islam had
been a constant feature of European politics throughout the Middle
Ages. From the eighth century Arabs and Berbers controlled not
only the whole of North Africa, but much European territory as
well, in Spain, Portugal and Sicily. This long contact with the Arab
world formed part of the education of a rough and primitive Europe.
European art and industry owe much to the Arabs. Greek science
and learning found their way to mediæval Europe—in so far as
they were known at all—largely through Arabic translations. Even
the elaborate conventions of late mediæval chivalry were to some
extent imitated from Arab customs and Arab romances. With all
this, however, there was no fusion between the two civilisations. In
places where Christian and Muslim lived together on the same soil,
a contemptuous toleration might be offered by one race, in return
for payment of tribute by the other; but in general the line between
Christian and Muslim was clearly drawn and their normal relation
was war. So normal and habitual did this war-like relation become
that it seemed at times to lose some of war's bitterness and to take
on the conventions of the tournament; but some event, some change
in the balance of forces always occurred to renew the bitterness.

On the one hand, Muslim religious enthusiasm was strengthened from time to time by waves of reinforcement from Central Asia. These waves—of which the Ottoman Turks formed the last and most dangerous—kept the frontiers of Christendom in recurrent fear. On the other hand, the aristocracies of Western Europe, urged on by the Church, sought repeatedly to defend their territories and to recapture lost ground in the Crusades.

The Holy War against Islam was successful in recapturing, in the course of time, all the territories of Southern Europe which had formerly been Christian and Latin-speaking. Outside Europe, the Crusades made little impression upon the body of Islam. The mixture of motives among the Crusaders—religious zeal, personal love of adventure, hope of trade or of plunder, desire for reputation—made for disunity. The European nations never embarked on Crusades as organised states. Even those armies led by kings or by the Emperor in person were bound together only by feudal and personal ties. No kingdom in Western Europe had then an organisation capable of administering distant possessions; only the knightly Orders had the organisation, and their resources were inadequate. The conquests of the Crusaders—such, for instance, as the Latin states established after the first Crusade—disintegrated of themselves, without needing the pressure of Muslim counter-attack.

The antipathy between Latin and Greek Christians further weakened the crusading movement and diverted it from its main object, the capture of the Holy Places. The fourth Crusade, without seriously harming the Infidel, dealt a crippling blow against the much battered Byzantine Empire. Its chief beneficiaries were the Venetians, firmly established as the carriers of oriental merchandise from the Levant ports to the insatiable markets of Western Europe. With its principal bastion thus weakened, the crusading movement was thrown upon the defensive—an unsuccessful defensive in the face of the advance of the Ottoman Turks in the fourteenth century. It was not the efforts of the Crusaders, but the military successes of a rival conqueror—Timur—further east, which arrested the conquests of the Turkish Sultan Bayezid and granted Europe a short respite at the end of the fourteenth and beginning of the fifteenth centuries. The fall of Constantinople and the conquest of the Balkans by one Asiatic conqueror or another was clearly only a matter of time. The crusading nations of Western Europe had neither the strength, the will nor the unity to prevent it.

Despite the failures and defeats and the ultimate collapse of the crusading movement in the Near East, the idea of the Crusade persisted in all the countries of Europe which were in contact with

Muslim peoples. In those countries, crusading was in the blood of most men of gentle birth and adventurous impulses. This was nowhere more true than in Portugal, a poor and small country which owed its national existence to a long Crusade, and in Spain, where the Crusade was still going on. The frustration of the greater Crusade in the Near East led to attempts to find means of attacking Muslim power elsewhere. If not by land, then by sea; if the Infidel were proof against frontal attack, he might be outflanked or taken in the rear; and if the strength of the European Crusaders were inadequate, then alliances might be sought with other Christian princes. Stories were current of powerful though forgotten Christian kingdoms, perhaps in East Africa, perhaps somewhere in Asia. If communications could be established with the East, moreover, by some route outside Turkish control, then the oriental trade which supplied the Turk with much of his wealth might be diverted into Christian channels.

War and trade went hand-in-hand in the later Crusades. Portugal possessed a long ocean sea-board, a considerable fishing and sea-faring population, and a powerful commercial class largely emancipated from feudal interference. Portuguese shippers were able and eager to graduate from an Atlantic trade in wine, fish and salt to more widespread and lucrative ventures in slaves, gold and spices. The first and obvious object of Portuguese military and commercial expansion was North-West Africa, where a large and prosperous Muslim community was living almost within hailing distance. Operations began with a sea-borne attack on the town and fortress of Ceuta in 1415.

The expedition to Ceuta was a genuine Crusade, though with a limited and temporary object. It was organised by King John I, partly in order to strike a blow against the Moors by sacking one of their principal harbours—the key to the Mediterranean, Azurara called it; partly to give his sons, who were candidates for knighthood, an opportunity to win their spurs in real battle rather than in the artificial fighting of the tournament. The operation was a brilliant success and the fall of Ceuta struck a resounding blow throughout Europe. Its importance lay, not merely in the fact of the capture, but also in the bold decision to hold the place with a Portuguese garrison instead of razing it to the ground. A European state was undertaking, as a State, the defence and the administration of an overseas possession in Muslim territory. Ceuta offered many possibilities: a base for advance into Morocco, or for an attack on Gibraltar, the other great Moorish fortress in the western Mediterranean; the incentive, and probably to some extent the information, needed for the beginning of systematic African exploration and trade. With the capture of Centa the crusading movement passed from its mediæval to its modern phase; from a war against Islam in the Mediterranean basin to a general struggle to carry the Christian faith and European commerce and arms round the world.

The most outstanding figure in the first stages of Portuguese—and indeed of European—overseas expansion was Prince Henry of Portugal, nicknamed by English historians 'the Navigator'. Prince Henry served with great distinction at Ceuta, not only at the capture in 1415, but also three years later when he relieved the Portuguese garrison from a Moorish counter-attack. He was intimately concerned with the Crusade in both its forms: its older, narrower form of a Mediterranean war against Moor or Turk, and its newer form of a world-wide strategy for the encirclement of Islam, a strategy in which the exploration of the West African coast and the Atlantic islands was only the first move. He is chiefly remembered now as the organiser of African exploration; but for him the African voyages were a new means to an old end. His many-sided character summed up the best of old and new in the changing times in which he lived. He was both recluse and man of affairs; ascetic and generous host; Governor of the knightly Order of Christ, and friend of seamen, merchants, cartographers, instrument makers; a Catholic Christian of deep and orthodox piety, and a patron of much that was new in learning and science. Under such leadership the beginning of European expansion by sea was no sudden break with the past, but the natural outcome of centuries of crusading hope and frustration.

I

THE TOOLS OF THE EXPLORERS

(i) *Charts*

If it was the crusading spirit, in the person of Prince Henry, which set the Portuguese upon a career of overseas expansion, crusading zeal was not, of course, the whole story. Courage, discipline and organising ability played their part; and besides these moral considerations must be set another group of factors, commercial and above all technical, which contributed to the astonishing achievements of the Portuguese in two continents in the course of a single century. As an introduction to the narrative of Portuguese exploits, some account must be made of these factors; of the tools available in the fifteenth century for making Prince Henry's dreams a reality.

One of the most obvious characteristics of European civilisation is its preoccupation with technical problems and its mastery of a wide range of mechanical devices. Technical skill and the ability to turn theoretical knowledge to practical material ends have been major factors in the extension of European influence round the world, and have forcibly, though not always favourably, impressed all the peoples with whom Europeans have come into contact. This characteristic has been most marked in the last century or century-and-a-half; but it has been an important element in the whole history of European expansion. The scientific knowledge of the time, whether the result of genuine discovery or of the revival of classical knowledge, was turned very quickly to practical account.

In the story of exploration and overseas expansion, three branches of technical development proved to be of the first importance. One was the study of geography and astronomy and its application to the problems of practical navigation. The second was ship-building and the development of skill in handling ships. The third was the development of fire-arms and in particular of naval gunnery. In the first two, at least, of these branches of skill the people of Western Europe drew upon the knowledge either of their classical predecessors or of their Eastern neighbours, but applied that knowledge in ways undreamed of by its original discoverers.

It was common knowledge among educated people in the fifteenth century that the earth was round. This, like so much of the academic knowledge of the Middle Ages, was derived at many removes and by devious ways from the Ancients. The Hellenistic world had produced a whole school of systematic mathematicians and cosmographers: Hipparchus, Eratosthenes, Marinus of Tyre, and the geographer Strabo, to mention only the better-known names. Eratosthenes had actually calculated the circumference of the earth and arrived at a surprisingly accurate answer. Both Eratosthenes and Strabo left recognisable descriptions of the continents which they knew. Beyond the limits of the knowledge or report of their own day they were content to leave a blank and to assume a vast encircling ocean. The culmination of ancient geography, however, was in the compilations of the Hellenised Egyptian, Ptolemy, who wrote about A.D. 130, at the time of the greatest extent of the Roman Empire. Ptolemy left two principal works, an Astronomy, more commonly known by its Arabic title, the *Almagest*, and a descriptive *Geography* of the known world of his time.

The heirs of the Greeks in geography, as in many other sciences, were the Arabs. Most Arab cosmographers preferred Ptolemy's description of the world to those of his predecessors because it was more complete and more symmetrical. Preoccupied as they were, also, with astronomy and astrology, the Arabs made great use of the *Almagest*, but neglected the *Geography*, which remained a forgotten work throughout most of the Middle Ages. The Arabs added little to geographical knowledge by actual exploration, because their great journeys both by land and by sea were in regions already roughly known to the Ancients—the Mediterranean and the countries bordering the northern Indian Ocean. They believed the Atlantic to be unnavigable, and had a deep superstitious dread of the 'green sea of darkness', which they communicated to Western Europe. On the other hand, Arab geographers contributed a mass of ingenious theory about the hypothetical centre of the habitable world and the symmetrical arrangements of the continents round it. A complex mixture of the *Almagest* and Arab theory, passed on in Latin translation, supplied the basis of academic geography in late mediæval Europe.

Upon this basis European scholastic writers, from Roger Bacon to Pierre d'Ailly, constructed systematic treatises embodying a mass of scriptural references, legends and travellers' tales. Of these works the most influential, and one of the last, was the *Imago Mundi* of Cardinal Pierre d'Ailly, a mine of quotations from Greek, Latin and Arab authorities, a work of immense erudition, but completely remote from sea-faring reality. It is one of the very few books which are known to have been studied by Columbus.

The *Imago Mundi* was written in 1410. That year was notable also for the recovery by Western Europe of Ptolemy's *Geography*, which at last emerged from its long obscurity in the form of a Latin translation. This example of the steady revival of classical learning was obviously of immense significance in the development of scientific geography. It was not, however, an unmixed encouragement to explorers; for though Ptolemy's work was a great improvement upon current theory, it contained a number of ancient errors of fact. Ptolemy's map of the world was a reasonably accurate picture of the Roman Empire and adjacent countries; but outside those limits Ptolemy had filled in the blank spaces of earlier maps from his own imagination. He invented a vast southern continent joined at one end to Africa and at the other to China, making the Indian Ocean a land-locked sea; he declared the whole southern hemisphere to be unnavigable because of the heat; and he contradicted Eratosthenes' estimate of the circumference of the globe, substituting his own, which was an under-estimate of about one-sixth. Ptolemy's *Geography* exercised an immense though not undisputed influence for at least two hundred years; and much of the history of the early discoveries was the story of practical men who proved Ptolemy to be wrong.

From all this it is clear that even the best academic geography of the early fifteenth century bore little relation to the experience of practical sailors. In so far as it was known to seamen at all, it was an almost paralysing discouragement from exploration by sea; and the *mappa-mundi*—the theoretical world-maps based upon it—were useless for the purpose of ocean navigation.

Fifteenth-century sailors, however, did not go to sea without charts. From the thirteenth century at least, there had existed in the Italian and Catalan ports a school of professional hydrographers who drew *portolani*—charts intended for use at sea, based on sailing experience and owing little to academic science. The original designers of these beautiful late mediæval charts are unknown; but the designs were good, and like many devices used by practical men they were repeated, with additions but without fundamental changes, from one generation to another. They consisted of free-hand but clear and accurate outline drawings of coastlines with headlands, rivers and harbours marked. The later ones were supplied with compass roses and were criss-crossed with a network of rhumb-lines or loxodromes serving to show the courses from place to place. Most of them covered the Mediterranean and the Black Sea; some extended to northern Europe and included a truncated Africa. They were drawn on a consistent distance scale but not on a consistent projection; it was not until the sixteenth century that Mercator devised his famous projection with its technique of showing both latitude and longitude as straight lines. The working accuracy of the portolans, therefore, was good only for comparatively short passages. They could be used, within limits, for dead-reckoning at sea, but not for fixing the position of a ship out of sight of land.

When the Portuguese embarked on their voyages to the South, charts of the portolan type began to be drawn of the African coast, and it became necessary to have a reference scale against which to mark the features of the coast as they were discovered. In the later fifteenth century, Portuguese cartographers began to add to the network of loxodromes on their charts a single meridian, usually that of Cape St Vincent, extending across the chart from North to South and marked in degrees of latitude. Latitude could be measured only by celestial observation; and in the early fifteenth century the rudimentary astronomical knowledge of Europe was the preserve of the learned. To the practical sailor it was still a closed book in an unknown language.

The learned world of Western Europe derived its knowledge of astronomy from the Arabs, chiefly through Portuguese and Italian Jews, who were the natural intermediaries between Christendom and Islam at that time. The Arabs' purpose in studying the heavens was not primarily navigation, but cosmography and astrology, and for these purposes they relied somewhat uncritically upon Ptolemy's *Almagest* and upon the works of early Indian astronomers. They supplemented Ptolemy, however, by a great deal of painstaking observation spread over many centuries. They identified and named many stars and studied their tracks relative to the earth. Some of this astronomical knowledge affected the practice of eastern navigators. Arab sailors regularly sailed by the stars—that is, they shaped their course by the bearings upon which prominent stars were known to rise and set. Such a system was reliable only in the latitudes where no great variation occurred in the azimuths of the appropriate stars, and where the regularity of the seasonal winds made it possible to sail great distances upon a prearranged course. Some Arab *baghlas* cross the Indian Ocean in the same manner today. What was more important, fifteenth-century Arab sailors possessed rough methods of observing the altitude of heavenly bodies as a help in fixing their position. Portuguese navigators, in solving far more difficult problems than the Arab sailor ever had to face, needed similar help from the men of science. One of the tasks of Prince Henry and his successors was to bring together for this purpose the seafaring and the learned worlds of Europe.

The easiest and most obvious star to use in observing latitude is the Pole Star, because it is always aligned within a few degrees of the earth's axis. The altitude of the Pole Star—the vertical angle between the star and the observer's horizon—gives the observer's latitude. The first recorded observation of latitude from the altitude of the Pole Star in a European ship was in 1462, two years after Prince Henry's death, but there is no doubt that his captains had been experimenting with the method for some years before that. As exploration went on, however, the Pole Star sank towards the horizon; and as they approached the equator the explorers lost sight of it altogether. The difficulty of observing latitude in the southern hemisphere was a serious stumbling-block to fifteenth-century navigators; but in 1484 a group of astronomers consulted by King John II produced the suggestion that latitude might be calculated from observation of the height of the sun at midday. For this calculation, the navigator would need tables of the sun's declination—the distance of the sun's zenith north or south of the equator at noon on any given day. Here the Arab study of the heavens was of use, again through the medium of the Jews. An almanac containing declination tables had been compiled in 1478 by a Portuguese Jew named Abraham Zacuto, who was professor of astronomy at Salamanca, and who later, upon the expulsion of the Jews from Spain, came to Lisbon as astronomer-royal. Zacuto's tables were written in Hebrew. John II's committee had them translated into Latin, and shortly afterwards (the date is uncertain) they were published in Portuguese as part of a general treatise on navigation entitled *O Regimento do Astrolabio*. The publication of this, the first practical manual, marked a revolutionary advance in the science of navigation.

It is characteristic of the Portuguese attitude that they did not neglect to send an expedition to Guinea in 1485 to test the new methods of observing latitude.

To sum up: at the beginning of the fifteenth century the navigator had no means of finding his position once he lost sight of land, and consequently he took care as a rule not to lose sight of land. At the end of the century, an intelligent and literate navigator had at his disposal several methods of discovering his latitude; he had an agreed estimate of the geographical length of a degree of latitude—eighteen Portuguese leagues, an error of only four per cent; and he had charts on which his observations could be plotted. He had no means of finding his longitude—that was a more difficult problem, not satisfactorily solved until the eighteenth century; but by a combination of observed latitude and dead-reckoning he could keep track of his position tolerably well. Much of the mediæval navigator's horror of the open sea had thus been dissipated. All this achievement was due to an unprecedented combination of sea experience and academic knowledge; and the methods really worked. In Vasco da Gama's great voyage to India, which closed the century, there was no more dramatic feature than the accuracy of his navigation and of his first landfall on the South African coast.

It would be wrong, however, to assume that even at the end of the century the taking of celestial observations was a commonplace among sailors. On the contrary, it was a considerable event, and when successful was recorded with pride in the journals of voyages. Celestial navigation did not yet form part of the professional training of ships' officers, and even practised experts needed favourable conditions in order to achieve reliable results.

A word about instruments: European ships had carried compasses at least since the thirteenth century, and by Prince Henry's day the compass had developed from a magnetised needle floating on a chip of wood in a bowl of water, to a pivoted needle swinging above a compass-card marked with the four cardinal 'winds' and the thirty-two points which we know. Gimbals were introduced about 1500. The existence of variation was known, but the extent of variation in different longitudes was a matter of conjecture. The compass gave the navigator his course to steer, and from a sketchy knowledge of ocean currents he estimated his course made good. Speed made good was largely a matter of guess-work. The earliest form of log was a piece of wood, made fast to a long line knotted at regular intervals; when the log was streamed, the speed at which the knots ran out over the stern was timed with a diminutive sandglass. This 'chip' log, however, was an early sixteenth-century invention; in the fifteenth century, the navigator studied the behaviour of his ship along known stretches of coast, and so learned to guess his speed by watching bits of wood or other flotsam floating by. For dead-reckoning, he used a chart of the kind already described, usually drawn on parchment. He had no pencil, and pricked holes in the chart with his dividers instead—as slovenly navigators still do. Having no parallel ruler, he lined up his straight-edge with the nearest convenient loxodrome on the chart.

For celestial navigation the principal requirement was an instrument for measuring the altitude of heavenly bodies. The cross-staff and its refinement the back-staff were sixteenth-century inventions; the standard fifteenth-century device was the astrolabe. The elaborate brass astrolabes, both oriental and European, which survive in many museums, were designed to work out a variety of academic astronomical and astrological problems, and were certainly never used at sea. The astrolabes actually used by the Portuguese navigators were much simpler, the simplest form being a disc marked in degrees with a swivelling pointer mounted at the centre. The pointer was fitted with aperture sights, one at each end. The instrument was suspended vertically from a ring at the top. The observer held the ring in his left hand, and with his right aligned the sights with his chosen star. He then read off the angle shown by the upper end of the pointer. Obviously it was extremely difficult to hold the instrument steady on the deck of a rolling ship. The Portuguese explorers of the African coast preferred, whenever possible, to take their sights ashore. They stood in towards the coast, anchored, pulled ashore, and hung their astrolabes from tripods set up on the beach. From this position they took their noon sights and worked out their latitudes with, on the whole, surprising accuracy.

For taking sights at sea the fifteenth century produced a slightly handier instrument, a rudimentary quadrant. Although lighter and simpler than the astrolabe, it worked on a similar principle and cannot have been much more accurate when the ship was rolling. Columbus on his first voyage took both an astrolabe and a quadrant with him. He used the quadrant regularly to take Pole Star sights. There is no record of his taking sun sights, or of his using the astrolabe at all. On his second voyage he seems to have left it behind.

(ii) *Ships*

At the beginning of the fifteenth century the seaborne trade of Europe was carried in ships markedly inferior in design and workmanship to the vessels used in many parts of the East; but at the end of the sixteenth century the best European ships were the best in the world. They were, perhaps, less handy and less weatherly than the junks of the China seas, but in general, in their combination of seaworthiness, endurance, carrying capacity and fighting power, they proved superior to anything else afloat, and they have retained that superiority ever since. The importance of this factor in the story of European expansion is obvious. As in their navigation, so in the design of their ships, European seafarers first borrowed and imitated, then developed and improved their borrowings beyond recognition.

Much of the trade of fifteenth-century Europe was carried in galleys. Oared vessels were preferred in the Mediterranean for their reliability and their independence of the wind. Galleys won the battle of Lepanto, as late as 1570; they did not disappear altogether until the eighteenth century; but they were obviously unsuitable for exploration or for any kind of deep-sea work, and for trade in rougher water the maritime nations of Europe had already by 1400 considerable numbers of sea-going ships which used oars only in emergency, if at all. Some of these ships were surprisingly large; they were heavy, usually clinker-built, and very broad in the beam. Their build gave them stability, and enabled their topsides to be built up to a considerable height. For purposes of war, additional height was given by fitting raised 'castles' fore and aft to accommodate cross-bowmen and the light artillery of the time, and to facilitate boarding. These castles in the Middle Ages had usually been temporary structures, and ship-building towns often had guilds of castle-wrights, specialised craftsmen whose trade was to convert merchantmen into men-of-war by fitting them with castles. Already by 1400, however, the practice was growing of building a permanently raised fo'c'sle and poop as part of the structure of big ships, a practice carried to extremes in the early sixteenth century.

The European ship of about 1400 was almost always square-rigged, and the limitations of square-rig accentuated the clumsiness of the hull. Unless the wind were astern or nearly so, the ship tended to make excessive leeway, and a head wind kept it in harbour. Square-rig, on the other hand, has one important advantage: it enables the total sail area of a ship to be divided into a large number of units, each of a size which can be easily handled. A square-rigged ship, therefore, can carry a very large area of canvas with safety; and square-rig proved the most satisfactory rig for big ships. In 1400, however, the principle of breaking up a ship's canvas area for ease of handling was in its infancy. A few big ships had two or even three masts; most had only one. Each mast carried a single sail laced to a great yard. Topsails, in later years the main driving sails of all big ships, were introduced after 1400 and at first were of pocket-hand-kerchief size.

In general, the sailing ship of Western Europe, though it had attained considerable size by 1400, was still a clumsy and primitive affair. It could carry large numbers of men or a bulky cargo for comparatively short passages with a fair wind. It was wholly unsuitable for following the windings of strange coasts, exploring estuaries, meeting the dangers of shoals, lee shores and head winds. The square-rigged ship—the *nau*—played no considerable part in the early discoveries. The Portuguese preferred a borrowed alternative, the lateen caravel—a highly individual craft which betrayed Asiatic influence in its every line. Here, too, the Arabs were their teachers.

The deep-water trade of the Indian Ocean from Suez to Malabar was in the fifteenth century almost an Arab monopoly. Taking advantage of the alternating monsoons, Arab shipmasters maintained a regular seasonal trade then, as they do today. The ships now engaged in the trade, especially the largest type, the Persian Gulf *baghlas,* show unmistakable European influence in the transom stern, with its elaborate carved ornament, and in the method of fastening the hull with iron spikes. In the fifteenth century all Arab ships were probably double-ended, and their planks were sewn edge to edge with coir fibre. The characteristic features of design—the 'grab' bow, the deep keel, the absence of raised fo'c'sle, the long poop —are pure Arab and were much the same then as now. The hulls were stoutly built, and then as now constructed mainly of Malabar teak, a more durable material than European oak.

In rig, as in hull design, the larger Arab ships have probably changed little since the fifteenth century. They have usually two masts with a pronounced forward rake. Each mast carries a single lateen sail; a triangular or nearly triangular sail, the leading edge of which is bent on a long yard hoisted obliquely to the mast. The lateen sail is the special contribution of the Arabs to the development of the world's shipping; it is as characteristic of Islam as the crescent itself. It is also a very efficient general-purpose rig. The qualities of any sail when beating to windward depend largely on its having the leading edge as long and as taut as possible; these qualities are supplied in the lateen sail by the long yard, and by simple adjustments the set of the sail can be altered to suit almost any wind conditions.

The Arab lateen rig has two serious disadvantages. One is the difficulty of going about; the yard has to be carried over the masthead, a complicated and awkward manœuvre. Under Indian ocean wind conditions it is rarely necessary to go about; and if he must alter course, the Arab ship-master will usually wear round. The other disadvantage is more fundamental: the size and weight of the spars. The design of the lateen sail is such that only one sail can be carried on each mast. The sails must therefore be large ones, and very long spars are needed to carry them. The length of the main yard is usually about the same as the overall length of the ship. It is made of two or three lengths of teak fished together, and is naturally very heavy. Obviously there is a limit to the size of spar which can be handled, and this factor limits the size of the ship. In spite of these disadvantages, however, Arab ships in general are handy, reliable and seaworthy craft; and those used for crossing the Indian Ocean in the early fifteenth century were far better designed than any purely European type in use at the time.

The lateen-rig and Arab notions of hull design spread into the Mediterranean as a result of the Muslim incursions, and were no doubt studied and imitated by the Portuguese in the course of their long conflict with the Moors of North Africa. The Portuguese retained, however, European methods of hull construction and fastening. As a consequence, the caravels in which Prince Henry's captains made most of their voyages differed in rig and design, though not in construction, from the square-rigged ships of the rest of Western Europe, and resembled in most respects the *Sambuks* which may be seen in any Red Sea harbour today.

Unlike the Arabs, however, the Portuguese did not rest content with the lateen-rig as they found it. The caravel did not remain a constant type; it developed steadily through the fifteenth century, as long-range exploring voyages revealed its defects. In the first place the difficulty of going about was overcome by shortening the yards, by setting them more nearly upright, and fitting them more snugly to the masts. This made it unnecessary to carry the yard over the masthead when going about, the yard being kept always on the same side of the mast, as in modern Mediterranean lateen boats. The loss of sail area caused by these changes was compensated by stepping a mizen mast, thus giving the caravel three masts instead of two.

The number of masts could not be increased indefinitely, however, and as the Portuguese captains ventured farther and farther from home, they began to find their caravels too small for the long voyages they had to make and the stores they had to carry. We have seen that a purely lateen-rigged ship cannot be increased in size beyond a certain point without loss of efficiency, and that the Arabs never found a solution of this problem. Towards the end of the fifteenth century, the ship designers of Portugal and Spain found a solution by combining the advantages of European square-rig with those of the oriental lateen in one vessel. This vessel was the *caravela redonda*, the square-rigged caravel, employed in most voyages of discovery in the late fifteenth and early sixteenth centuries. It had a kind of primitive barquentine rig, usually with square sails on the foremast—course and topsail, and later, top-gallant also. It retained

lateen-rig on main and mizen. The distribution of square and lateen
sails varied to some extent; the main-mast might be square-rigged
like the fore; and sometimes there were four masts, two of them
square-rigged. The square-rigged caravel retained the advantages of
the lateen when sailing close-hauled, and its greater spread of canvas
made it much faster when running.

The successful combination of square- and lateen-rig in one vessel was an event of the first importance in the history of European
shipping. It quickly extended not only to light vessels of the caravel
type, but to big ships also. By the early sixteenth century ships all
over Europe were normally fitted with one or more lateen sails. The
famous *Henri Grace à Dieu*, for instance, built to Henry VIII's
orders, although she retained the traditional hull design with enormous castles fore and aft, was of composite rig. She had five masts,
three square-rigged, the other two lateen; and though a very large
ship for her day, she was a reasonably fast sailer, could sail reasonably close to the wind, and was much easier to steer than she would
have been with square-rig alone.

The spread of the combined rig made possible a change in the
nature of exploring voyages. The early voyages on the west coast of
Africa were reconnaissances carried out by one or two caravels. The
later voyages, to India and across the Atlantic, from the last decade
of the fifteenth century, were made by powerful fleets including both
ships and caravels, the two types being by then capable of sailing in
company in all reasonable weathers; and the caravels came to be
employed, to some extent, as escorts for the larger cargo-carrying
ships.

It should be clear from all this that fifteenth-century Spanish and
Portuguese caravels were stout, handy and sea-worthy. They were
not the tubs or cockle-shells of popular history, and all but the
smallest were fully decked. They must, nevertheless, have been extremely uncomfortable. There was no provision of sleeping accommodation except the cabin for senior officers aft. A caravel had no
raised fo'c'sle, as a rule, and the fore-peak was filled with cables and
gear. There were no hammocks; those were an invention of the
American Indians. The ship's company slept on the deck or the
hatch-covers as best they could, and in bad weather down below.
That must have been singularly unpleasant; apart from rats and
cockroaches, all wooden ships leak to some extent, and pumping
out seems to have been a daily routine for the morning watchmen.
In bad weather there was probably no dry space in the ship. Cooking
was carried out in an open fire box in the bows, the bottom of which
was filled with sand. On the sand a wood fire was built when the

weather allowed. Food consisted of salt beef and pork, beans, chick-peas and ship's biscuit; except, perhaps, for a short-lived supply of fresh provisions for the after-cabin. It is interesting to notice that in Lisbon there were extensive biscuit ovens belonging to the Crown and only a stone's-throw from the royal palace. Water in cask soon becomes foul, and large quantities of wine were carried, the normal daily allowance per man being about one-and-a-half litres. The wine and water casks provided the principal ballast of the ship.

Columbus's fleet on his first voyage carried ninety men, of whom perhaps forty sailed in the *Santa Maria*. Considering that she was not much bigger than a Brixham trawler, this was overcrowding by modern standards; but since she carried no soldiers she was much less overcrowded than the warships of the time. The ship's company seem to have worked a two-watch system, the watches being much the same as they are now. The master and the pilot were the two officers in charge of the two watches. At that time ships intended for sea-fighting often carried a sailing-master who worked the ship and a pilot who navigated her, as well as the captain, who commanded her. The captain was not necessarily a professional seaman; in a man-of-war he was more often a soldier. It was only with the development of naval gunnery that soldiers were ousted from sea-going command.

(iii) *Guns*

Sea-fighting in the later Middle Ages was chiefly a matter of laying alongside and boarding. Galleys were sometimes fitted with rams, but it is unlikely that they ever did much damage with them. Sailing ships designed for fighting were built up fore and aft, originally in order to give their boarding-parties the advantage of height. These superstructures proved so convenient for purposes of cabin accommodation that they remained a distinctive feature of most big ships long after the original reason for them had disappeared. In the fifteenth and sixteenth centuries the castles and fighting tops in big warships were manned by soldiers, who were carried for fighting and who were a body distinct from the sailors who worked the ship.

It is difficult to say who first introduced ship-borne artillery, and when. Probably the Venetians first used it in the fourteenth century in their incessant quarrels with the Genoese. By the middle of the fifteenth century most big European fighting ships carried guns—usually small forged pieces mounted in the castle structures fore and after. They were intended to supplement cross-bow and arquebus fire in raking the enemy's upper deck. The Portuguese caravel, however, widely used for exploration and for escort duties in hostile seas, had no raised fo'c'sle, only a modest poop, and no fighting tops. In caravels, the guns were mounted in the bows and on the poop, and if greater fire power were required, ranged along the waist firing over the gunwale. Towards the end of the fifteenth century, embrasures were cut in the gunwales for the guns to fire through. This practice of broadside fire, once introduced, quickly spread to the great ships of all the European nations. The substitution of cast for built-up barrels also produced a type of artillery too heavy to be housed in the castle structures, and in the early sixteenth century, shipwrights hit upon the revolutionary idea of mounting guns between decks and piercing the ship's side with ports. At first these ports were small round holes allowing no traverse for the guns, so that all fire had to be point-blank; but in the course of the sixteenth century they developed into big square ports with hinged scuttles which could be secured against the sea in bad weather. The guns were then fitted with wedges for purposes of elevation and tackles for training, and continued to be so fitted until the nineteenth century.

The development of broadside fire affected not only naval tactics, but ship construction. The mounting of large numbers of guns along the ships' sides increased the top weight and the strain on the ships' timbers. The desire to counteract these tendencies, among other reasons, produced the 'tumble-home' of the sides, which became a characteristic feature of wooden warships from the sixteenth century onwards. In extreme cases, especially in big Spanish ships, the width of the upper deck was only about half the water-line width. When two such ships lay alongside one another, their gunwales were so far apart that boarding was extremely difficult; a circumstance which helped to emphasise the importance of gunnery in sea-fighting.

The Portuguese, the leaders of all Europe in nautical matters in the fifteenth century, seem to have been the first people to recognise the gun and not the foot-soldier as the main weapon in naval warfare, and to use guns against the enemy's ships rather than against his men. Significantly, the first battles fought on the principle of sinking ships by gunfire were fought in the Indian Ocean, not in the Atlantic or the Mediterranean.

2

'CHRISTIANS AND SPICES'

(i) *The sea crusaders*

The capture of Ceuta placed the Portuguese in possession of much information about Africa which was not available to other Europeans. In Ceuta, Prince Henry must have heard of the caravans which crossed the desert to Timbuktu and returned to Morocco with ivory and gold dust obtained by barter from the Negroes of the Niger basin. Whatever the precise nature of this information, it led to an increasing preoccupation with Africa. In 1419, the year after his second expedition to Ceuta, Prince Henry accepted the more or less sinecure office of Governor of the Algarve, the southernmost province of Portugal. He retired from the Court and from politics and began to build his little settlement of Sagres on Cape St Vincent, the rocky tip of south-west Portugal. Here, overlooking the Atlantic, he held his small court, consisting largely of men who used the sea or were interested in seaborne trade or discovery. Not only sailors, but astronomers, ship-builders, cartographers and instrument-makers, many of them Italians, were invited to visit Sagres, to work at Prince Henry's expense and under his direction. From 1420 the Prince began to send out from the nearby port of Lagos a series of small but regular expeditions to explore the west coast of Africa.

There was no premature flowering of the Renaissance on Cape St Vincent; Prince Henry, though a highly significant figure, was also a staunchly conservative one. Azurara, the contemporary chronicler of Prince Henry's achievements, lists the motives which impelled him to organise these voyages, and states that the first was a desire to know what lay beyond the Canaries and Cape Bojador. There was no suggestion, however, of a scientific or disinterested curiosity;

the purpose was practical and is further explained by the second motive, the desire to open profitable new trades, presumably with the producers of gold. Azurara insists, to be sure, that trade must only be with Christian peoples, whom the explorers hoped to encounter beyond the country of the Moors. This was standard mediæval doctrine. Although some purists considered *all* trade to be incompatible with knighthood, it was thought legitimate by many to deprive the infidel of resources for making war by indirect means if direct means failed. The third, fourth and fifth objects mentioned by Azurara were all conventional crusading aims: to investigate the extent of Moorish power, to convert pagans to Christianity, and to seek alliance with any Christian rulers who might be found. The long-lived Prester John legend, fed no doubt by rumours of the Coptic Kingdom of Abyssinia, was by this time localised in Africa; and the hope of contact with some such ruler connected African exploration with the older Mediterranean crusade. The last, and strongest, motive attributed by Azurara to the Prince was his desire to fulfil the predictions of his horoscope, which bound him to 'engage in great and noble conquests, and above all . . . to attempt the discovery of things which were hidden from other men.' This, too, was a conventional late mediæval attitude, and a reminder that in Prince Henry's day astronomical knowledge was still more commonly applied to fortune-telling than to navigation. In general, it was with conventional mediæval motives and mediæval intellectual equipment that Prince Henry embarked on the task of organising the exploration of West Africa.

Progress in the early years was extremely slow. It was fourteen years before a European ship ventured beyond Cape Bojador, the first major landmark on the West African coast. Cape Bojador was a formidable obstacle to sailing ships hugging the coast. The sailors were held back, also, by the old terror of the green sea of darkness, inherited from the Arabs; and by the fear that the tropical sea might prove to be boiling hot or that the tropical sun might turn them all into Negroes. But Prince Henry was both patient and insistent, and eventually a young squire named Gil Eannes took a caravel round Cape Bojador and proved that the sea to the south of it was much the same as the sea to the north. After 1434 exploration went on smoothly at a much more rapid pace.

The second psychological obstacle to be overcome was the scepticism of those who thought that no profit could come of the African expeditions. These sceptics were confuted in 1441, in which year a caravel brought back from the coast south of Cape Bojador a small parcel of gold dust and a little party of Negro captives. In the

next five years down to 1446 Portuguese ships brough back nearly
a thousand slaves, either captured or bought from the coastal chiefs
between Cape Bojador and Cape Blanco, which latter Cape was
reached in 1442. These captives were well treated by the standards
of the time. They were carefully instructed in the Christian faith and
some of them were employed as interpreters in subsequent expeditions. The trade in slaves became so extensive that in 1448 Prince
Henry ordered the building of a fort and warehouse on Arguim
island, in the bay formed by the curve of Cape Blanco. This Arguim
warehouse was the first European trading factory overseas.

When the prince found that the discoveries which he organised
had considerable commercial value, he secured from his brother the
king the sole right to visit and trade with the Guinea coast. At the
same time he tried to make the Guinea venture attractive on religious grounds, by obtaining from successive Popes grants of plenary
indulgence to all who took part in African exploration; and received
also papal confirmation of his own monopoly of the work of converting the African Negroes to Christianity. This habit of appealing
to the Pope for confirmation of overseas discoveries was an important feature of the diplomacy of the time, and produced awkward
complications later, when Spain and other nations entered the field
of maritime exploration. It stood Prince Henry in good stead and was
an integral part of his policy—the policy of drawing the Portuguese
away from Iberian and European politics, and interesting them in
activities where their skill as seamen and ship builders enabled
them to outstrip far stronger nations.

Prince Henry used his monopoly generously, and financed foreign
as well as Portuguese traders and explorers. The Venetian Cadamosto, for example, made voyages under Prince Henry's licence
to the Atlantic islands and West Africa as far as the Gambia, in
1455 and 1456. Cadamosto wrote journals which contain vivid descriptions of the places he visited, observations on trade and navigation, and a wealth of entertaining details such as the most convincing early description of a hippopotamus and some useful hints
on how to cook ostrich eggs. This garrulity on Cadamosto's part is
a welcome change from the silence of his Portuguese contemporaries.
The official Portuguese policy was one of secrecy concerning discoveries, and this secrecy grew closer and stricter after Prince
Henry's death.

Prince Henry died in 1460. Of the many contemporary tributes
to his work, two are outstanding. One is Azurara's *Chronicle of the
discovery and conquest of Guinea*, a panegyric, but a sincere and
convincing one. The other is an indirect tribute—the world-map

of Fra Mauro. This famous map, of large size and exquisite workmanship, was drawn in the Camaldolese Convent of Murano in Venice, to the order of the King of Portugal, Prince Henry's nephew, Affonso V. Cadamosto is said to have helped in the drawing of Africa. The map was completed in the year before Prince Henry's death; its most arresting feature is its record of the discoveries made in his lifetime, from Ceuta to Sierra Leone. There is no evidence in any of the contemporary accounts that Prince Henry ever contemplated the possibility of reaching India by sea. India in his day was known to Europeans only by hearsay. Its products were known; and the commercial advantages of direct contact were obvious, should such contact ever prove feasible. It was only in the last years of Prince Henry's life, however, that his captains discovered the easterly trend of the Guinea coast south of Sierra Leone, giving rise to the hope that Africa was a peninsula, in spite of the teaching of Ptolemy. Naturally, as this possibility opened up, it added a new and powerful motive for exploring the African coast.

(ii) *The Cape of Storms*

Although African exploration began as Prince Henry's private hobby, it had the sympathy and probably the support of at least one of his brothers, the regent Prince Pedro, and during the lifetime of the two princes it became for a time a matter of considerable national interest. After Pedro's death in 1449, however, the pace of exploration slackened; and when Prince Henry himself died and his monopoly passed to the Crown, a pause ensued of over ten years without any major discovery. The next important date was 1471, when Fernando Po discovered the island which bears his name near the mouth of the Niger, and discovered also the sharp southerly trend of the African coast just north of the equator. This must have been a severe disappointment to men who had hoped that India was just round the corner; and four years later, in 1475, a still more serious interruption occurred, in the shape of war with Spain, arising out of a Portuguese claim to the Castillian throne. In this war, which was bitter and destructive, Portugal was defeated and Isabella was confirmed as Queen of Castille; but as often happened, the Portuguese, having lost the war, won the treaty, at least from the colonial point of view. Among its many clauses, the treaty of Alcaçovas in 1479 confirmed to Portugal the monopoly of the trade, settlement and exploration of the West African coast and the possession of all the known Atlantic islands except the Canaries, which remained to

Spain. The first of the long series of European treaties regulating colonial spheres of influence was thus a diplomatic triumph for the Portuguese.

Two years later Affonso V died, to be succeeded by John II, one of the ablest and least scrupulous princes of his century, a competent geographer and an enthusiast for discovery. One of his first acts was a decree which laid down that all foreign ships visiting the Guinea coast might be sunk or captured without inquiry. If captured, their officers and men were to be thrown to the sharks, notoriously plentiful in those waters. Partly in order to enforce this legislation, partly to facilitate trade and to defend the traders against native attack, John II embarked in 1482 on the building of a second fortress and warehouse on the African coast, on a more ambitious scale than the old one at Arguim. The site chosen was at Elmina on the Bight of Benin. The stone used in the construction of the keep was all shipped out from Portugal, with a small army of workmen. Elmina soon became the naval and commercial capital of the African discoveries and the centre of a thriving trade in slaves, ivory, gold-dust and Malaguette pepper—the coarse pungent pepper of the Guinea coast. Part of the profit of this trade was applied to financing a hydrographical office and a school of navigation.

With the financial resources of the Crown at his disposal, and with none of Prince Henry's patience with unprofitable servants, John II secured rapid results in African exploration. The most distinguished of the captains whom he employed were Diogo Cão and Bartholomeu Dias. In 1483, Cão reached the mouth of the Congo and explored some way up the river. In 1486, in a second voyage, he sailed as far as Cape Cross. In the following year Bartholomeu Dias left Lisbon on the famous voyage which was to solve the problem of the southern extremity of Africa.

Very little is known about Dias. There is no portrait of him in existence and no detailed and reliable account of his voyage. He was probably a man of quite humble origin, like most professional seamen of his day, but he must have been a very capable navigator, for Vasco da Gama ten years later was able to follow his directions with accuracy and success. We know that his experience was employed in designing and fitting out the ships of Vasco de Gama's fleet.

Dias's achievement was more than a mere continuation of southerly sailing. The Cape of Good Hope is not the southerly extremity of Africa. The southernmost point is Cape Agulhas, considerably farther east. Between them lie False Bay and a difficult stretch of coast with a current setting from east to west. But Dias was a fortunate as well as a capable seaman. He was in the latitude of Walfisch

Bay, or thereabouts, when his ships were caught by a northerly gale which blew them south under reduced canvas for thirteen days out of sight of land. When the wind moderated Dias squared away on the port tack in order to regain the West African coast; but he had already passed the Cape without knowing it, and eventually made his landfall at Mossel Bay on the Indian Ocean. Dias himself would have liked to explore farther; but his men were tired and frightened and inclined to be mutinous and his two caravels were small and ill-provided for sailing farther into the unknown. He had left his storeship at Walfisch Bay; and so he agreed to return there to rejoin it. It was on the homeward passage, therefore, that Dias first sighted the great cape which he had been seeking. According to the chronicler Barros, he first called it the Cape of Storms; it was the king who, upon Dias's return, renamed it the Cape of Good Hope.

It was to be for some years the cape of hope deferred. The way to India seemed to lie open; but voyages to India were not to be undertaken by small European kingdoms without due thought. The king's attention was taken by political troubles and succession disputes; and to confuse the situation, in March, 1493, Columbus's *Niña* put into the Tagus, having returned—so her company said—across the Atlantic from easternmost Asia. If Columbus were right, the best part of a century of Portuguese exploration would be wasted; the prize which seemed within the Portuguese grasp would fall undeserved into the hands of Spain; inevitably there would be trouble. In fact, Columbus's assertions did not deceive the Portuguese for long; but they led to long and intricate negotiations, designed by the Portuguese to prevent or to limit further Spanish exploring. It was not until 1495 that the decision was taken to send a fleet to India; and not until 1497 that the fleet actually sailed.

Vasco da Gama's fleet consisted of four sail: three ships, square-rigged with lateen mizens, and a lateen caravel; he was to trade, therefore, and not only to explore. Apart from its results, the voyage was memorable in itself as a magnificent feat of seamanship. Profiting by Dias's experience, da Gama stood far out across the Atlantic until the trade belts were reached and passed; thus avoiding the Doldrums and making by far the longest passage yet made by a European ship out of sight of land. This was the course which generations of later Indiamen were to follow; a bold course then, when celestial navigation was in its infancy.

Da Gama touched at several places on the East African coast for water and fuel, and at the port of Malindi he picked up a Muslim pilot, Ibn Majid, as luck would have it one of the leading experts of his day in celestial navigation. With Ibn Majid's help he

navigated across the Indian Ocean to Calicut, one of the main spice
ports of the Malabar coast. His reception there was not particularly
promising. The Portuguese trade goods—mostly trinkets and
woollen cloth—were unsuitable for the Indian market; the local
Hindu ruler at Calicut was naturally unwilling to give up his profitable Arab connections, and the resident Arab merchants put every
pressure upon him to refuse facilities to the Portuguese. Nevertheless da Gama, with great difficulty and great persistence, collected
a quantity of pepper and cinnamon. With this cargo he cleared for
home; and the long story of European intrigue with the native
princes of India was begun. During his voyage, which lasted over
two years in all, da Gama had spent more than three hundred days
at sea, and had lost over a third of his company, probably as the
result of scurvy.

(iii) *The spice trade*

It is a commonplace of economic history that the farming communities of Europe, down to the late seventeenth century at least, suffered
from a chronic shortage of winter feed for cattle. Large numbers of
beasts had to be slaughtered every autumn, and the meat preserved
for winter consumption by being salted or pickled. Hence the constant and insatiable demand for spices as condiments and pre-
servatives. Salt was the commonest and cheapest preservative
(though not particularly cheap by modern standards) and much of
the salt supply of Western Europe came from Portugal. Apart from
salt, the preservative spices were all produced in tropical countries:
pepper, the commonest spice, in India, the East Indies and (a very
inferior sort) West Africa; cinnamon in Ceylon, nutmeg and mace
in Celebes and other East India islands, whence they were shipped
from the port of Macassar. Ginger is a Chinese product, though an
inferior kind was also grown in Malabar. The most valuable preservative spice—cloves—came from the most restricted producing
area, a few small islands in the Molucca group, including Tidore,
Ternate, Amboina and the Banda islands. To complete the list of
eastern trade goods, it is convenient to group together with spices
certain other products which commanded high prices in Europe
and which went there by the same routes: Chinese silk; Indian cotton
cloth; rhubarb, grown in China and much prized as a medicine; and
precious stones of various kinds—emeralds from India, rubies from
Tibet and sapphires from Ceylon.

The development of the spice trade in the fifteenth century was closely bound up with the expansion of Islam, both west and eastward, at the expense both of Christian and Hindu. The Ottoman Turks were terrorising Eastern Europe. Other central Asian peoples were pressing into India. A series of foreign Muslim dynasties had long been established at Delhi, and a string of loosely organised Muslim sultanates ruled the west coast as far south as Goa. Only in the south the wealthy and powerful kingdom of Vijayanagar survived as the principal stronghold of Hindu power. At the same time Islam was expanding by sea. Arab colonists had long controlled the towns and trade of East Africa as far south as Mozambique. Muslim traders were spreading their religion through the East Indies and establishing trading principalities. Petty sultans, often Malay in race, usually Muslim in religion, set up as merchant princes in the principal spice-producing islands. Wherever the European Christians went in the East they found that the Muslims had gone before them, and by 1500 both the production of spices and the trade in spices were largely in Muslim hands.

A considerable part of the trade between East and West in the Middle Ages had been carried across Asia overland. As far as Western Europe was concerned the activities of the Turks greatly reduced the importance of this route. It is with the seaborne Eastern trade that we are primarily concerned. At its eastern end, the trade was handled by the Chinese, whose junks collected the cloves, mace and nutmeg of the East Indies and carried them to the great Malayan port of Malacca. From Malacca across the Bay of Bengal to India, the trade had fallen by 1500 into the hands of Muslim merchants, whether Indian, Malay or Arab. In India, the Far Eastern cargoes, together with the cinnamon of Ceylon and the pepper of India itself, were sold in the spice ports of the Malabar coast—Cochin, Calicut, Cananore, Goa—and farther north in the ports of Gujerat, particularly Diu. The population of these ports was mainly Hindu, though some of them, including Diu and Goa, had Muslim overlords. Their trade with the rest of the Indian Ocean littoral was largely handled by the Arabs and by Muslim peoples subject to them. The merchant houses of Arabia, Egypt and East Africa maintained warehouses and resident factors, paying the local rulers for the privilege. To Malabar they brought horses from Mesopotamia and copper from Arabia. From Malabar their dhows cleared with immensely valuable cargoes for the harbours of the Red Sea and the Persian Gulf, whence the spices having been carried overland to Alexandria or the Syrian ports, and having paid heavy tolls in Cairo or Baghdad, were bought by Venetian merchants for distribution throughout Europe. The costs of the trade were enormous;

but so were the profits. It was said that a merchant could ship six cargoes and lose five, but still make a profit when the sixth was sold.

Until the Portuguese reached India, the Far East had been known to Europeans mainly through the accounts of thirteenth-century Franciscan missionaries, such as Carpini and William of Rubruck, who had visited the dominions of the Tartar Khans, and of that incomparable traveller and observer, Marco Polo. These men travelled from Europe to Asia by overland or partly overland routes. Naturally, therefore, although the Portuguese intention was to open a trade with India by sea, John II did not overlook the possibilities of exploration by land as a means of obtaining information and establishing preliminary contacts. In the fourteen-eighties a number of explorer-ambassadors were sent to various places in the East to discover what they could about India, and if possible to establish relations with 'Prester John'. The most successful of these Portuguese travellers was Pedro da Covilhã, who left Lisbon in 1487, the same year that Dias sailed on his voyage to the Cape. Covilhã travelled ostensibly as a merchant—he spoke Arabic—via Cairo to Aden, where he shipped in an Arab dhow to Calicut and made a reconnaissance of the ports of the Malabar coast. From there he returned in another Arab ship to East Africa, where he visited a number of Arab towns, and then made his way back to Cairo. Subsequently Covilhã succeeded in reaching Abyssinia, and spent the last thirteen years of his life there; but before leaving Cairo for the second time, Covilhã found a messenger to take a report of his journey to John II. In 1495, therefore, the planners of Vasco da Gama's expedition had before them not only Dias's report of the sea route as far as the Great Fish River, but also Covilhã's account of the harbours and trade of the Malabar coast. Da Gama thus knew what to look for; and when he returned with the news of success, in 1499, the Portuguese government was ready with a detailed plan for an organised commerce, involving the establishment of factories in the Malabar ports and the despatch of annual fleets under royal charter.

A fleet sailed in 1500 under Pero Alvárez Cabral, who upon his arrival at Calicut, quarrelled with the resident Muslim merchants and with the Hindu authorities, and established a factory at the rival port of Cochin, farther down the coast. The third Indies fleet, commanded again by Vasco da Gama, sailed in 1502. This was a powerful and well-armed force, fourteen sail in all, and with it da Gama carried out a heavy bombardment of the town of Calicut, an important event in the history of naval gunnery as well as in that of Indo-European relations. Da Gama also fought and won the first naval pitched battle in the struggle for control in the East, against a fleet equipped by the Malabar Arabs. The Arab fleet, though numerous, apparently had no manœuvring organisation, and its gunnery was poor. It was almost annihilated by a much smaller Portuguese squadron which had been trained to use its guns and to manœuvre as a squadron.

These early voyages to India demonstrated that a Portuguese fleet, if properly armed and well commanded, could defeat any Asiatic fleet in the open sea. Further proof was provided by the decisive victory of Almeida, the first Portuguese viceroy, over the combined Egyptian and Gujerati fleets off Diu in 1509. It remained true, however, that in fair and open trade the Portuguese could not compete with the Arabs or rely upon the goodwill of the local Hindu rajas. European manufactures were crude and unattractive in Eastern eyes; and the local rulers could not be expected to see, in the tatterdemalion crews living a crowded squalor in their sea-stained ships, the fore-runners of a power which was to conquer half the East. Momentarily dangerous the Europeans might be; but in the eyes of a cultivated Hindu they were mere desperadoes, few in number, barbarous, truculent and dirty. It became clear that in order to profit fully by their monopoly of the Cape route the Portuguese would have to destroy the Arab trade in spices by force of arms at sea. The task of planning and executing this naval war fell to the ablest sea commander of his day, Affonso d'Albuquerque.

(iv) *The Portuguese Indies*

The Portuguese plan in the East was never one of mere commercial competition. They never proposed to undersell Arab and Venetian merchants by flooding Europe with cheap spices; nor could they have done so if they had wished. The relation between Portuguese and Arabs from the start was war, embittered by all the circumstances of racial and religious hatred.

When Albuquerque first went out to India in 1503, the Portuguese settlements consisted merely of warehouses where the royal factors and the agents of the Lisbon merchant houses chaffered for spices in the squalor of the water-front bazaars. Every year or every other year, armed fleets sailed from Lisbon to collect the spice cargoes. The tenure of the factories and the continuance of the trade depended on the forbearance of the local rajas. To convert this precarious foothold into an enduring maritime and Christian Empire, the Portuguese needed a permanent fleet in the Indian Ocean. For this, they required a secure naval base with adequate facilities for provisioning

and refitting their ships, and a reserve of seafaring men on the spot
to replace the appalling losses caused by climate and disease among
their ships' companies. In addition, they needed fortresses, supported by mobile cruiser squadrons, commanding the termini and
clearing-houses of the Indian Ocean trade routes. They had to
change an entirely seaborne interloping commerce based on Lisbon,
into a chain of permanent commercial and naval establishments
covering the whole of the Middle East. This was the costly and ambitious plan which Albuquerque forced on a parsimonious government, when in 1509 he became governor-general in succession to
Almeida.

The base which he selected was Goa, a big and prosperous city
built on an island, with a sheltered harbour, one of the centres of
the ship-building industry of the Malabar coast. It is still a Portuguese possession, and still builds sailing ships of local teak. The capture of Goa was a bold and difficult operation and its retention
against the armies of the Sultan of Bijapur a lesson in the effects of
sea power. The channels which separate Goa from the mainland are
shallow and could be forced—were indeed forced several times—
by Indian cavalry. Horses will not breed in South India; they had to
be imported. Albuquerque's fleet cruising off Goa could deny to his
enemies this essential weapon and could confine the supply of horses
to princes friendly to the Portuguese.

Goa was taken in 1510. Already before that, Albuquerque had
established fortresses off the Arabian coast. One was the island of
Socotra off Cape Gardafui, intended as a base for forays into the Red
Sea—waters then unknown to Europeans—and for the interception
of spice cargoes consigned to Jeddah and Suez. Aden would have
been a better base; but Albuquerque's attempts on Aden were
failures, and Socotra also was abandoned after the first few years.
The other Arabian fort was in a much more important place—
Hormuz, an island at the mouth of the Persian Gulf and one of the
greatest markets in the world for Eastern products. Hormuz occurs
constantly in the literature of the sixteenth and seventeenth centuries
as a synonym for oriental wealth and splendour. It was the capital
of an independent sultan and itself a considerable naval power. The
Portuguese took it by an astonishing combination of bluff and seamanship, with only six ships.

Established at Hormuz and Socotra, the Portuguese commanded
the western extremities of the Arab trade routes. With a major base
at Goa and minor bases strung along the Malabar coast, they could
control the trade of the west coast of India and in due course extend
their power to the coast of Ceylon. It only remained for them to

capture a base farther east, to enable them to stop or control Muslim trade across the Bay of Bengal. The obvious place was Malacca, commanding the Strait through which all intercourse with the Far East had to pass. Albuquerque took Malacca in 1511, risking his hold upon Goa in order to do so, since the monsoon which took him to Malacca made it impossible for him to return until five months later. The siege strained his resources in men and ships to the utmost and Goa all but fell in his absence. The gamble succeeded; with Malacca, the western terminus of Chinese trade, in their hands, the way to the Far East lay open to the Portuguese. The first Portuguese trader to reach a Chinese port put into Canton in 1514; this was the first recorded European visit to China since the 'Tartar peace'. In due course the Portuguese secured tacit permission for a warehouse and settlement at Macao, a little downstream from Canton, and began to take a direct part in the trade from China to Malacca.

More important still, from their own point of view, at about the same time the first Portuguese ships reached the Moluccas, the famous spice islands which had been the ultimate goal of almost all their exploration. The Portuguese entered into treaty relations with the Sultan of Ternate, the principal clove-producing island, and built a fortified warehouse there for collecting the cloves. No doubt they intended to turn the place into an outright possession like Goa and Malacca as soon as their strength allowed.

In all this breath-taking story, no single factor is more remarkable than the soundness of Albuquerque's strategic judgments, based, as they must have been, upon grudging and incomplete information. He was perhaps the first sea commander to appreciate fully the complex relationship between a fleet and its bases, allowing for the additional complication caused by seasonal changes of wind. He calculated with careful accuracy the necessary proportion of escorts to merchant packets, neither wasting cargo space nor leaving valuable cargoes unprotected. In order to assert the Portuguese crown monopoly of the spice trade, he established a kind of navicert system, whereby only those ships carrying certificates from the captain of a Portuguese port were free from molestation. His depredations against Arab spice shipments raised the prices which the Venetians had to pay at Alexandria; while his countrymen at Ceuta could, when they wished, close the Straits of Gibraltar to Venetian ships. By all these means, spices and other valuable cargoes destined for Europe by sea were soon almost confined to Portuguese bottoms and carried via the Cape, to the great profit of those engaged in the trade, and in particular of the Portuguese Crown.

Albuquerque never undertook the responsibility and expense of territorial acquisitions unless they contributed directly to the needs of the fleet. In all the ports held by the Portuguese, fortress areas were set apart containing the dockyards, the warehouses, the barracks and the living quarters of the European residents. Captains of ports seldom intervened in administrative matters outside the fortress areas, except in the event of serious risings or riots threatening Portuguese interests. Even at Goa, the Hindu and Muslim communities were necessarily governed mainly through their own headmen. Obviously if the Portuguese had tried, as the Spaniards did, to train their newly conquered subjects in European ways, the attempt would have failed; but even the will was lacking. Few Portuguese governors deviated from a strictly commercial policy. There was plenty of missionary activity, of course; to this day there are in South India and Ceylon considerable numbers of Christians with Portuguese baptismal names—Catholic Christians, distinct from the much older Nestorian communities. But they are only a fraction of the population. On the whole the Portuguese showed remarkable obtuseness in dealing with native religions. They regarded the Hindu, in the early years at least, as a kind of Christian, and were outraged when he refused to behave as such. The Muslim was always a potential enemy. Albuquerque himself, alone among Portuguese governors, tried to establish peaceful relations with the resident Muslims and to attach them to his person; but even he could not ruin their trade with one hand, and convert them to Christianity with the other.

3

THE NEW WORLD

(i) *The Fortunate Isles*

Prince Henry of Portugal was not only the instigator of exploring voyages along the west coast of Africa, with India as the ultimate goal; he was also the patron of westward exploration into the Atlantic, for related but somewhat different reasons. The Portuguese were naturally jealous of their African and later their Indian trade monopoly, and relentlessly attacked any foreign shipping which they encountered on the high seas near the African coast. The chief interlopers, or suspected interlopers, were Spaniards. Throughout the fifteenth century in every quarrel, diplomatic or otherwise, between Spain and Portugal, colonial possessions and overseas trade were always among the grounds of contention.

The bitterness of these early colonial disputes arose not only from Portuguese fear of Spain at home, but also from the fact that, throughout the exploration of West Africa, the Portuguese had upon their seaward flank a group of islands, some of which were occupied and all of which were claimed by Castille. These were the Canaries—the Fortunate Isles which in Ptolemy marked the western edge of the habitable world. Portugal tried often but without success to establish a counter-claim to the Canaries. As the century wore on and other groups of islands were discovered, the Portuguese took care to occupy those islands before Castille or any other power could do so. The Atlantic islands were important for three reasons: firstly in themselves, since many of them were fertile and became extremely productive; secondly as bases and harbours which, if occupied by foreigners, could be used for attacks on Portuguese trade in West Africa; thirdly, towards the end of the century, as ports of call in possible attempts to reach Asia by sailing west.

Four main groups of islands were involved: the Canaries, the Madeira group, the Azores and the Cape Verde islands. From the early fourteenth century at least, Europeans knew of the existence of all these groups except the last, the Cape Verde Islands, which were first sighted either by Cadamosto or a Portuguese contemporary. Some of the more ambitious portolan charts of the fourteenth century marked the Canaries and Madeira and even indicated the Azores, though vaguely and inaccurately. There were many stories of voyages made to various islands by Catalans, Frenchmen and even one Englishman, Machin by name, who was supposed to have sailed to the Azores accompanied by an abducted bride. Many of these stories were romantic legends. It was not until the fifteenth century that any systematic attempt was made to occupy or even to explore the islands, and the colonisation of Madeira and the Azores in Prince Henry's day may fairly be called a re-discovery.

The first settlement of Porto Santo and thence of Madeira began in 1420 under charter from Prince Henry. After the inevitable initial hardships the islands quickly became productive and prosperous, and yielded a handsome profit to the settlers, to those who traded with them, and indirectly to their overlord, Prince Henry. The earliest important trade was the export to Portugal of high quality timber for furniture and the beams of houses. Next in time, but financially more important, was the sugar trade. The demand for sugar all over Europe was large and growing. Prince Henry caused sugar cane to be brought from Sicily and planted in Madeira. In 1452 he put up the capital to build the first windmill for crushing the cane, and from that time Madeira sugar began to be sent, not only to Portugal, but to all the major ports of Europe. To Prince Henry also, Europe owes the introduction to Madeira from Crete of the Malvoisie grape, from which the characteristic dessert wines of Madeira are made. When Brazilian sugar captured the Portuguese market a century or so later, wine became the chief business of Madeira and has remained so ever since.

Prince Henry's claim to Madeira was based on the solid ground of prior occupation backed by Papal grants, and was never seriously disputed. The settlement of the Canaries was a much more contentious and complicated story. Unlike Madeira, the Canaries were inhabited by a primitive but numerous and warlike people, the Guanches; the conquest and colonisation of the islands—there are seven important ones—was a long and arduous business. The Castillian Crown secured some sort of papal title to the Canaries as early as 1344; from the first years of the fifteenth century various adventurers planted settlements in Lanzarote, Ferro and Fuerteventura, and did homage for them to the King of Castille. Prince Henry's attempts on the islands began with two expeditions, in 1425 and 1427, to Grand Canary, then unoccupied by Europeans; these expeditions were beaten off by the natives. Next, in 1434, he extracted from the Pope a bull authorising him to settle those islands not actually occupied by Spain; but the King of Castille protested, and two years later the bull was withdrawn. In 1448, the prince purchased rights in Lanzarote from the principal settling family, and sent an expedition which succeeded in occupying the island. There ensued a period of unofficial but savage local war, punctuated by intervals of comparative peace. It was during one of these intervals that Cadamosto visited the Canaries and touched at both Spanish and Portuguese islands. His journal shows the Canaries developing economically along the same lines as Madeira, with sugar, wine and wheat as the principal products.

The privateering war among the islands was swallowed up, in 1475, by the succession war between Spain and Portugal; in the treaty of Alcaçovas the Portuguese Crown abandoned all claims in the Canaries, while the Spaniards undertook to respect the Portuguese monopoly in the three other island groups. The Spaniards had taken Grand Canary during the war. They conquered Palma in 1490 and Tenerife in 1493, so that by the end of the century the whole archipelago was in their hands and has remained so to this day.

One result of this conquest was that Portuguese ships sailing to Lower Guinea tended to pass well to seaward of the Canaries in order to avoid Spanish privateers, and to make their first call at the Cape Verde Islands. This group, lying several hundred miles offshore, was first discovered either by Cadamosto or by Diogo Gomes in 1555–6; the islands were soon settled, and their small harbours achieved a modest prosperity by selling provisions to ships in the Guinea trade. The Cape Verde Islands were less useful as a port of call on the return passage, because of the difficulty of sailing directly to Portugal in the teeth of the north-east trades. Instead, ships returning from Guinea—or, later, from India—passed close to Cape Verde itself and then steered north or nor'-nor'-west until they found a westerly wind to take them down to Portugal. This usually involved a call at yet another island group, the Azores. The systematic exploration of the Azores had begun in the fourteen-thirties, and seven of the islands had been discovered by 1439, in which year Prince Henry granted charters to various people to settle. Settlement went on steadily from that time, and considerable numbers of sheep were taken out by Prince Henry's orders. The two westernmost island, Flores and Corvo, were not discovered until after the middle of the century. Corvo is in the latitude of New York, and once there, the Portuguese were well on the way to America.

Throughout the fifteenth century, then, sailors were discovering islands in the Atlantic. There was no apparent reason why the discovery of fresh islands should not go on indefinitely. Optimistic explorers saw an island in every cloud bank, and peppered the Atlantic charts with imaginary islands: Brazil Rock, not removed from Admiralty charts until 1873; St. Brendan's Isle, off Ireland; most famous of all, Atlantis or Antilla, the isle of the seven cities, where, it was rumoured, seven Portuguese bishops had migrated with their flocks during the barbarian invasions, and where their descendants lived in piety and great prosperity ever since. It was one of the dreams of fifteenth-century sailors to rediscover this mythical land, its Christian people and its gold. Probably in the Atlantic harbours of Spain and Portugal there were men who claimed to have seen Antilla; perhaps on the western horizon at sunset, only to miss it by an error of steering during the night. It was into such a world of sailors' yarns, where anything might happen, that Columbus came peddling the 'enterprise of the Indies' round the courts of Europe.

(ii) *Discovery*

Much ink and erudition has been expended on the problem of what Columbus hoped to find, and probably the exact answer will never be known. He was a secretive man, and kept the details of the 'enterprise of the Indies' to himself. The agreement which he made with the Crown of Castille in 1492 provided that he was to command an expedition, fitted out largely at the expense of the Crown, 'to discover and acquire islands and mainland in the Ocean Sea'. If successful, he was to receive rewards, listed in detail in the agreement. Years before, as early as 1484, he had sought a similar agreement with the Portuguese Crown, but his proposal, after a fair hearing, had been rejected. The next eight years had been spent in attempts to interest one government or another in his project—India or Antilla —until at last Columbus managed to enlist the support of a great officer of state, Luis de Santangel, keeper of the privy purse to the King of Aragon and treasurer of the *Santa Hermandad*. Santangel himself raised a considerable part of the money needed to finance the enterprise. Through his good offices the consent of the Spanish monarchs was secured, and once committed, they agreed to all Columbus's terms. Three vessels were chartered or otherwise made

available for the expedition: the ship *Santa María* and two caravels
of which one, *Pinta,* was square-rigged. The other caravel, *Niña,*
was probably lateen-rigged originally, but was altered to square-rig
during the fleet's stay at Las Palmas in the Canaries on the way out,
apparently because Columbus found her to be under-canvassed. The
size of these vessels is a matter of conjecture. None of their actual dimensions are known. A ship's size at that time was usually reckoned
from the number of tuns of wine she could stow in cask. Measured
in this way, Columbus's caravels are reported to have been of about
sixty tons. The *Santa María* was larger, perhaps 100 to 120 tons. This
ancient capacity measure bears no exact relation to any modern
system of reckoning; and in modern gross tons the figures would
no doubt be rather smaller. Though small, the vessels were handy
and well found, especially the caravels. They were manned from
their home port of Palos by reliable crews with capable and experienced officers. Columbus himself possessed a rudimentary knowledge of hydrography and had served in Genoese and Portuguese
ships for some years. The voyage was to reveal him as a careful and
accurate, though not very up-to-date navigator. His observed positions were sometimes, it is true, wildly out; but his dead-reckoning
—which, in cases of conflict, he rightly preferred—had an uncanny
accuracy. He had a compass rose in his head. To picture him as an
unpractical mystic is mere caricature; to say, on the other hand,
that he knew his job and made full and careful preparations, is to
emphasise, not to belittle, the faith and courage which the 'enterprise of the Indies' demanded.

Apart from its terrifying distance out of sight of land, the outward
journey was prosperous. Columbus's course, due west from the
Canaries, passed along the northern fringe of the north-east trade
belt. The trades are not always reliable so far north, and September
is the hurricane season, so that Columbus was lucky to have a fair
wind the whole way out. Had he sailed in a Portuguese ship and
made the Azores his last port of call, he would have had westerly or
south-westerly winds to contend with, and might never have reached
America. As it was, after thirty-three days of uneventful sailing, the
fleet sighted the outer cays of the Bahamas.

Whatever Columbus's original objective may have been, there
is no doubt that he regarded San Salvador as an outlying island in
the archipelago, of which Japan was supposed to form a part—such
an archipelago as is marked, for instance, on Martin Behaim's 1492
globe. Columbus apparently reached this conclusion by combining
Marco Polo's estimate of the land length of Asia from east to west,
which was an over-estimate; the same traveller's report of the dist-

ance of Japan from the shores of Asia, 1,500 miles, a still grosser over-estimate; and Ptolemy's estimate of the size of the world, which was an under-estimate. He then assumed the length of an equatorial degree of longitude to be 10 per cent shorter than Ptolemy had taught and 25 per cent shorter than the true figure. Thus Columbus made the westward distance from Europe to Japan less than 3,000 nautical miles. The actual great circle distance is 10,600 nautical miles. According to Columbus's reasoning, San Salvador was very near to where Japan ought to be, and the next step was to find Japan itself.

With this object the expedition explored Santa María de la Concepción, which later and less pious sailors have renamed Rum Cay; the north-east coast of Cuba; and part of the north coast of Hispaniola, modern Haiti. In Hispaniola, prospects brightened, for the island yielded a little alluvial gold, and a number of gold nose-plugs, bracelets and other ornaments were obtained by barter from the natives. On the coast of Hispaniola, however, Columbus lost his flagship, wrecked apparently through negligence on the part of the officer of the watch. As a result, he decided to return home, leaving some of his men behind with instructions to build houses and search for gold-mines. The admiral himself proposed to come out again with a much larger fleet the following year.

On his return passage Columbus was again fortunate with his winds; whether by luck or good judgment, he decided to sail north or north-east as far as the latitude of Bermuda, where he was able to run down to the Azores before the prevailing westerlies. On nearing Europe, however, he ran into foul weather, and was compelled to put in for shelter, first in the Azores and then in the Tagus; and there, in a Portuguese harbour, he was naturally required by the King to explain his activities and his extraordinary claims—claims which, if substantiated, would strike a deadly blow at Portuguese ambitions.

John II was a competent geographer and was not impressed by Columbus's geographical reasoning. The Portuguese were sceptical about Italian exaggerations, and were in any case unwilling to believe that the new discoveries had any connection with Asia. Nor did Columbus's description of the primitive Arawaks tally with the legendary accounts of Antilla. Columbus, in fact, had discovered some new and apparently worthless islands in the Atlantic. The very fact of Spanish exploration in the Atlantic, however, was unwelcome. John II decided to lay claim to Columbus's discoveries, on the grounds that they came within the provisions of the treaty of Alcaçovas, that they lay close to the Azores, and might even be regarded as forming part of that group. It was to strengthen their case in negotiating against this claim that the Spanish monarchs applied for support to the only recognised international authority, the Papacy.

The Pope of the time, Alexander VI, was himself a Spaniard and for a variety of political reasons proved amenable to Spanish demands. In accordance with the wishes of Ferdinand and Isabella, as advised by Columbus, he issued a series of bulls, of which the first confirmed Spanish possession of the new discoveries; the second, the famous *Inter Caetera*, drew an imaginary boundary from north to south a hundred leagues west of the Azores and Cape Verde Islands, and provided that the land and sea to the west of this line should be a Spanish sphere of exploration.

John II had no intention of going to war over a few islands in the western Atlantic. He accepted the bull of demarcation as a basis for negotiation, and merely asked that the boundary line be moved two-hundred-and-seventy leagues west. The Spanish monarchs, secure in the delusions which Columbus had fostered concerning the western route to India, agreed; both sides must in any case have realised that so vague a boundary could not be fixed with accuracy, and each thought that the other was deceived. The treaty of Tordesillas was duly signed in 1494—a signal diplomatic triumph for Portugal, confirming to the Portuguese not only the true route to India, but the imaginary land of Antilla and the real land of Brazil; though probably that was not known, even in Lisbon, at the time.

Meanwhile, Spain and the rest of Europe outside Portugal accepted Columbus's own estimation of his discoveries. Ferdinand and Isabella believed his report and honoured all their promises. In 1493, before the conclusion of the Tordesillas negotiations, he was sent off in command of an impressive armada of seventeen ships, to establish a colony in Hispaniola, and using the island as a base, to continue his journey to Japan and India as he had promised.

(iii) *The interpretation of discovery*

Columbus on his second voyage spent about a year exploring the innumerable islands of the West Indies, but failed to find anything which remotely resembled India or Cathay. As governor of the new colony of Hispaniola he was a failure, and when he returned to Spain in 1496 the colony was in an uproar and the natives in revolt. His sovereigns fitted him out with a fleet for a third voyage, in which he discovered the island of Trinidad and the mouth of the Orinoco; but upon the renewal of trouble in Hispaniola, they not unreasonably superseded him as governor, and his successor sent him home in irons. He was allowed to make one more voyage of discovery at the royal expense in 1502. This fourth voyage, his most dangerous, and (for him) least profitable, revealed a long stretch of mainland coast in Honduras and Costa Rica, and yielded some gold; but by this time the Spanish monarchs were tired of Columbus's financial importunities. They refused to trust him again as an administrator, or to allow him to exercise any of his functions as admiral and viceroy; and in 1506 he died, a disgruntled, though still a wealthy man.

The disappointment of Columbus's second voyage naturally made responsible Spaniards suspect what the Portuguese had already assumed—that the new territories in the west were not part of Asia at all. Exploration outside the Caribbean increasingly confirmed this suspicion, as other European governments, particularly those of England and Portugal, became interested in western discovery in the north Atlantic. For the English this interest was not new. There had long been talk in west-country ports of islands to the west of Ireland, and attempts had been made to find them. From about 1490, something more than islands seems to have been involved; ships were reported to have left Bristol regularly, two or three each year, for unknown destinations in the western Atlantic. Possibly the Bristol men had found, and were exploiting, the Banks fishery; conceivably they had even reached the mainland coast. Nothing of this, apparently, was known in London. In 1488 Bartholomew Columbus had visited England, had tried to interest Henry VII in his brother's project, and had failed. In 1496, however, with knowledge of Columbus's discovery, Henry granted licence to explore in the western north Atlantic to John Caboto or Cabot, an Italian recently settled in Bristol. Nothing is known certainly about Cabot's intentions. His project was certainly much more than a fishing voyage, and more than a mere search for Atlantic islands. He may have learned, from Bristol seamen in the Iceland trade, something of the Vinland story—of the Norse wanderers who, centuries earlier, had found land to the south-west of their Greenland settlements; he may have heard of Scandinavian maps, or of actual English sightings of a mainland coast; he probably reasoned that such a coast, if it existed, must be a north-easterly extension of Asia, and proposed to follow it to the south-west until he reached mainland China, far to the west of Columbus's deceptive islands. The voyages which he made under the 1496 licence followed approximately the Viking route across the north Atlantic—though somewhat further to the south, since, so far as we know, he sighted neither Iceland nor Greenland—using the easterly winds which are frequent in early summer in those latitudes. Of a probable first, unsuccessful voyage in 1496, nothing certain is known. On the 1497 voyage, Cabot found land, possibly in Newfoundland, and after coasting for some distance returned to report. His last expedition, in 1498, apparently followed up the discovery, sailing past Newfoundland and Nova Scotia, as far as New England, perhaps further. The geographical results, with English banners attached, appear in de la Cosa's map. Cabot's ships brought back no silk or spices; his project was a commercial failure; he himself died on the voyage, and his English backers showed no further interest.

During Cabot's absence at sea Vasco da Gama's first voyage had revealed to an envious Europe the true route to India. No other European nation then cared to dispute the Portuguese monopoly of this route. On the other hand, neither da Gama's success nor the failures of Columbus and Cabot were enough to kill the hope of reaching Asia by sailing west.

It might still be possible to thread a way between the various masses of inhospitable land so far discovered. At worst, the New World, as it was coming to be called, had a certain value of its own. Columbus had found some gold; Cabot had found no spices, but had discovered a teeming fishery. In 1500 the Indies fleet of Pero Alvárez Cabral lighted upon the coast of Brazil and revealed the presence there of brazil-wood, an important raw material in the dyeing industry. Apart from immediate practical considerations, public interest in the New World was kept alive by a number of books on discovery published about this time in Germany and Italy. Books on discovery were among the best-sellers of the day. One of the most popular among them was a compilation called *Cosmographiae Introductio*, issued in 1507 by Martin Waldseemüller at St Dié in Lorraine. It included a Latin tract entitled *Quattuor navigationes*, which purported to be a letter from the Florentine Amerigo Vespucci, describing four voyages to the New World. The tract is now generally, though not universally, considered by scholars to be a forgery, in the sense that it was not written be Vespucci. It was a pirated account, partly based on genuine letters by Vespucci, partly invented; but the principal achievements which it described were real. Manuscript letters, subsequently discovered and more certainly attributable to Vespucci, though they contradict the printed tracts in important particulars, and record only two voyages, confirm the central facts. Vespucci was a business man, a man of substance, and indeed of some eminence in his native Florence. He first went to Spain in 1492 as a representative of the Medici, to supervise a number of marine supply contracts. His study of geography and navigation was a pastime, though one which, to judge from his letters, he pursued systematically and seriously. His residence in Seville gave him the opportunity to apply his theoretical knowledge to practical ends, and in early middle age he left his business concerns and became an explorer. Of the two voyages now generally accepted as authentic, the first, made in Spanish ships in 1499, was in the region visited by Ojeda, and for part of the way in company with him. It covered the coast from a point west of Cape São Roque, north-west and west to the Maracaibo lagoon. Vespucci's description of the drowned coast lands of Guiana and Venezuela is recognisably accurate. On this voyage, also, he made original and significant trials of a method of calculating longitude from the times of the conjunction of planets with the moon; a method too cumbersome to be of much practical use, though it persisted in manuals of navigational theory until the late eighteenth century. In 1501 Vespucci embarked on a second voyage, under Portuguese auspices and with knowledge of Cabral's sighting of the coast of Brazil. Vespucci reached the same coast in about 5° South and followed it in a south-westerly direction for more than two thousand miles, beyond the Río de la Plata, to a point—perhaps San Julián—on the coast of Patagonia; which coast he rightly reckoned to be on the Spanish side of the Line of Demarcation. Vespucci's two voyages, therefore, between them covered the greater part of the Atlantic coast of South America, revealed the continuity and vast size of that continent, and pointed the way which Solís and Magellan were later to take in seeking a western passage round it. The magnitude of these discoveries prompted Waldseemüller's suggestion that Vespucci's name should be given to the continent whose coast he had explored. The suggestion caught the popular fancy, and the name America quickly became attached to the southern continent. Later in the century, largely through Mercator's use of it, it came to be extended to North America as well.

Vespucci returned to Spain in 1505. He was appointed Pilot-major to the Casa de la Contratación at Seville, the first to hold that important and responsible office, in which he served until his death in 1512. His work was significant not only because of the extent of his discoveries, not only because of the publicity—unsought by him —which they received, but even more because of the soundness of his geographical knowledge and judgment. As an interpreter of discoveries he was unsurpassed.

After him all Europe recognised America for what it was, a new continent and a barrier—to everyone except the Portuguese, an unwelcome barrier—between Europe and Asia. The problem of finding a western passage to the spice islands, therefore, became not a problem of threading a way through an archipelago of islands, but one of finding a strait through a land mass whose dimensions from east to west were unknown. The belief that such a strait existed was strengthened by reports of the strong westerly flow of the Gulf Stream from the Atlantic into the Caribbean. Surely, it was argued, so great a volume of water must find an outlet somewhere.

Almost every European monarch at one time or another dreamed of finding a western passage and breaking the Portuguese monopoly of eastern trade. This universal ambition called for a new type of specialist—the professional explorer. The exploring activity of the early sixteenth century was dominated by a small group of men whose national allegiance sat lightly upon them and who were qualified and willing to undertake exploration on behalf of any monarch who would employ them. They were the maritime counterparts of the great army of mercenary soldiers who by that time were making a profession of the land fighting of Europe. Most of them were Italians, such as Vespucci himself, Verrazano and the two Cabots, father and son, or Portuguese such as Fernandes, Magellan and Solís. They served in turn the Kings of Spain, France and England and the Grand Signory of Venice. Against a background of growing jealousies and diplomatic cross-purposes they changed allegiance at will and carried from court to court information which their employers would have preferred to keep secret; yet such was the value set upon their knowledge that they were always welcome wherever they chose to settle. Only the Portuguese took care to employ their own nationals wherever they could; and consequently only the Portuguese succeeded in keeping their discoveries secret, until Magellan, in the sailors' phrase, blew the gaff.

(iv) *The division of the world*

The search for a western passage was encouraged, not only by a fallacious theory of ocean currents, but by a chance discovery in Central America in 1513. A Spanish adventurer named Balboa, resident in the island colony of Hispaniola, went exploring for gold with a band of followers on the mainland. He crossed the Isthmus of Darien and for the first time came within sight of the Pacific. Nobody until then had known how narrow a strip of land separated the two oceans. Balboa himself was not seeking a western passage, but his discovery naturally gave great encouragement to those who were.

Of the many expeditions which sought a passage through Central

and South America, all except one were failures—failures, that
is, in their immediate object; for the men who took part in them,
though they failed to find a strait, founded an empire. The story of
the Spanish conquest belongs to a later chapter; for the moment this
account of maritime discovery is concerned only with the solitary
success, the voyage of Magellan to the Pacific. The year 1519, in
which Cortés left Cuba to conquer Mexico, was also the year in
which Magellan left Spain to reach the East by sailing west.

The employment of Magellan by the Spanish Crown was the
climax to a long diplomatic contest. In 1494 the Spaniards had made
a bad bargain; for in allowing the bulls of demarcation to be superseded by the treaty of Tordesillas, they had unwittingly signed away
their right to explore Brazil. The Portuguese pursued their advantage
by securing papal confirmation of the treaty in the bull *Ea quae*
issued by Julius II, in 1506. That bull prevented any attempt to re-
vive Alexander VI's line of demarcation. By that time the regular
arrival of spice cargoes in Lisbon had revealed to the Spaniards
that they were being beaten in the race for the spice islands. They
sought, therefore, to use the treaty of Tordesillas to stay Portuguese
advance in the far East, hoping that a western passage would soon
be found. According to the Spanish interpretation, the line of demarcation established by the treaty ran right round the world, dividing
the world into two halves; in the one half, all unoccupied or heathen
lands were to be the prize of Portugal, in the other half the prize of
Spain.

The Portuguese, for their part, had no intention of accepting any
limitation of their eastward expansion. Even after their arrival in the
Moluccas, they had no exact means of determining the longitude of
the islands, nor did they know the size of the Pacific. If the Spanish
view of the demarcation treaty were accepted, it was by no means
certain that the Moluccas would fall on the Portuguese side of the
line; many contemporary charts, including some Portuguese ones,
placed them on the Spanish side. The Portuguese required an author-
itative pronouncement that the line of demarcation was confined to
the Atlantic; that it served simply to determine for each power the
route which must be followed to the Indies. Once again they sought
the support of the Papacy.

The amiable hedonist Leo X, a Medici, was interested in discovery and friendly to Portugal. The papal fancy had already been
pleased by the present of a performing elephant, sent to Rome by
Albuquerque, and in 1514 Leo acceded to all the Portuguese re-
quests. The bull *Præcelsæ Devotionis* gave papal blessing to discoveries and conquests which the Portuguese might make, and

granted to Portugal all lands which might be seized from heathen people, not only in Africa and India, but in any region which might be reached by sailing east.

Magellan, though a Portuguese, was impelled by circumstances to ignore the ruling of the bull. Before the date of its issue he had been in the East for some years, and had been present at the taking of Malacca. It is not certain whether he had actually visited the Moluccas, but some of his friends certainly had, and he knew the latitude of the islands. As for their longitude, he believed that the Moluccas lay reasonably near to South America and within what the Spaniards regarded as their sphere of influence. In that, of course, he was wrong. He also believed that a western passage might be found by following up the third voyage of Vespucci, to the extreme south of South America. In that he was right. When Solís made his voyage to the Río de la Plata in 1515, Magellan questioned the survivors and calculated from their reports that the south-westerly trend of the coast south of the estuary brought all that southern territory within the Spanish demarcation. In that he was also right. Obviously a successful voyage of discovery based on Magellan's reasoning would benefit nobody but the Spaniards; it was useless to expect the Portuguese government to finance such a voyage. Magellan accordingly turned to Spain, with an offer to discover wealthy islands in the East, within the Spanish demarcation and reached by an all-Spanish route.

In Magellan's agreement with the Emperor the Moluccas were not specifically mentioned. Magellan knew, though Charles V probably did not, that the Portuguese had already reached the Moluccas, and that the bull *Præcelsæ Devotionis* applied to the islands. Perhaps he hoped to find other, equally valuable islands in the same longitude; but the Moluccas were generally assumed to be his destination. His enterprise appeared as an act of aggression against Portugal and an act of defiance against the Pope. The Portuguese government tried by all possible diplomatic means to stop the expedition, but without success, and in September 1519 Magellan sailed from Seville with a fleet of five ships, laden with such goods as Portuguese experience had found suitable for trade in the East.

The events of Magellan's voyage are well known: the shipwreck and the mutiny off the coast of Patagonia; the discovery and the terrifying thirty-eight day passage of the strait which bears Magellan's name; the interminable crossing of the Pacific, which reduced the ships' companies to a diet of rats and leather; the inhospitable landings in the Ladrones and the Philippines and the death of Magellan and forty of his people in a local war. The skill, the en-

durance, and the achievement of Magellan before his death set him
with Columbus and Vasco da Gama as one of the greatest of explorers. But the voyage was only half completed. Sebastián del
Cano, the Spanish navigator upon whom the command devolved,
sailed south from the Philippines with only two ships remaining,
skirted the coast of Borneo, and in November 1521 reached the
Moluccas. The Spaniards were well received by the Sultan of Tidore,
upon whose territory they landed. They traded their merchandise
for cargoes of cloves and established a warehouse at Tidore, leaving
a small garrison to prepare for future expeditions. Then, since none
of his company felt inclined to face the dangers of Magellan's Strait
again, del Cano divided his forces. The *Trinidad* set off across the
Pacific for the coast of Mexico, and was captured by the Portuguese
before she was many days out. Del Cano himself eluded the Portuguese and took his battered *Victoria* through the Macassar Strait,
across the Indian Ocean, round the Cape of Good Hope, and back
to Spain with her precious cargo. She had been away for three years.
It was a prodigious feat of seamanship and del Cano shares with
Magellan the honour of this astounding voyage. He was the first
captain to sail round the world.

The wealth of information which this voyage produced can be
seen in the official Spanish map drawn by Diego Ribero in 1529,
embodying knowledge supplied by del Cano. Discovery apart, del
Cano's triumphant return produced two parallel sets of consequences. The first was a state of more or less open war between
Spaniards and Portuguese in the islands. The second was a fresh
series of outwardly amicable negotiations between Spain and Portugal in Europe. The second Spanish expedition to Tidore, in 1524,
was a disastrous failure; only one ship of a powerful fleet reached its
destination, and it became clear that whatever happened in Europe,
the Portuguese were in command of the situation in the East and
the value of the Spanish claim was beginning to depreciate. The
Emperor, at war with France and on the verge of insolvency, in 1527
conceived the ingenious idea of selling or pawning his claim to the
Moluccas before it should depreciate still further. In 1529, despite
the opposition of the Spanish Cortes, the treaty of Saragossa was duly
signed. By this treaty Charles pledged all his rights in the Moluccas to Portugal for 350,000 ducats in cash, and an arbitrary line of
demarcation was fixed seventeen degrees east of the islands. The
little garrison at Tidore, which had held out stubbornly against
heavy odds for more than five years, was instructed to hand over to
the Portuguese, and the Spaniards were given passages home in
Portuguese ships.

The treaty of Saragossa marked the end of a chapter in the story of discovery. Magellan's Strait was never afterwards used, by Spaniards or anyone else, as a regular channel of trade, and the route round Cape Horn is comparatively modern. Apart from a disputed frontier on the Río de la Plata, and the comparatively unimportant question of the Philippines, the colonial questions at issue between Spain and Portugal were for the moment settled. But neither the bulls nor the treaties in this long diplomatic contest could be held to bind third parties, and the search for the western passage was to be carried on by other nations.

4

THE SILVER EMPIRE

(i) *The Spanish conquest*

If the first two decades of the sixteenth century may be called the age of the professional explorer, the next three decades, from 1520 to 1550, were the age of the *conquistador*—the professional conqueror. In those years a few thousand down-at-heel swordsmen, themselves the product of the tradition of the Moorish wars, possessed themselves of most of the settled areas of both Americas and established the first great European land empire overseas.

Before 1520 most of the larger islands of the West Indies had been explored and a considerable number of Spaniards had settled, especially in Hispaniola and Cuba. These settlers imported cattle and horses, and Negroes to replace the dwindling native Arawaks, and set up as slave-owning ranchers. Their settlements were turbulent and unstable. Many of the settlers were soldiers who had served in Moorish or Italian campaigns; there was no congenial work for them in Spain, nor did they propose to work in the Indies. They would settle for a short time, and then desert their holdings to investigate a rumoured gold strike, or simply through boredom and restlessness.

Balboa's glimpse of the Pacific in 1513 encouraged some of these adventurers to join in the general search for a sea passage through Central America; at various points on the Gulf coast these explorers found gold and silver ornaments in use among the natives, and heard rumours of civilised city-dwellers living in the mountains inland. Scattered through tropical America, mainly in highland areas, there were in fact a number of distinct peoples, who, though lacking wheeled vehicles and beasts of burden, and using tools of wood or stone, had nevertheless achieved a remarkable skill in some of the arts, in sculpture and building, in agriculture and in handicraft industries, including the working of soft metals. Their principal settlements, adorned with stone or adobe samples and community-houses, were large enough to be called cities. In two centres at least —in Mexico and the central plateau of the Andes—warlike tribes had established themselves as overlords, exacting tribute and forced labour from subject peoples over a wide area; and had set up political organisations bearing a superficial resemblance to empires or kingdoms in the Old World sense. Among Spaniards, the wealth and power of these peoples lost nothing in the telling; and for pious Christians their religions had a horrible fascination, combining, as in some cases they did, messianic legends of strange beauty with revolting rites of human sacrifice and ritual cannibalism.

The speed with which the Spanish *conquistadores* seized the chief centres of American civilisation compares with the speed of Portuguese commercial expansion in the East; but the Spanish conquest achieved far more enduring results and its success is even harder to explain satisfactorily. The possession of firearms was an important but probably not a decisive factor. A ship carries its armament wherever it goes; but on land cannon had to be dragged over mountains and through swamps by human strength. The army with which Cortés invaded Mexico possessed only a few small cannon and thirteen muskets. Horses were perhaps more important than guns; but the Indians soon lost their fear of horses and even learned to ride them. Cortés had sixteen horses when he landed. For the most part his men fought on foot with sword, pike and cross-bow. They had the advantage of steel over stone; but they were not a well-equipped European army fighting a horde of helpless savages.

The Spaniards had unbounded courage and the discipline of necessity. They fought in brutally practical fashion, to kill and to conquer, unhampered by the Aztec convention of preserving live prisoners for sacrifice. They were able to exploit some of the legends and superstitions of their adversaries in such a way as to paralyse opposition, at least temporarily. They had the help of large numbers of Indian allies who—having never heard of King Log and King Stork—gleefully attacked their former overlords or rivals. Finally the Spaniards had the advantage of their truculent missionary faith: the Indian believed that his religion required him to fight and if need be to die bravely; the Spaniard believed that his religion enabled him to win.

The expedition destined for the conquest of Mexico, promoted by the governor of Cuba and commanded by Cortés, consisted of about six hundred men. Cortés landed near what is now Vera Cruz in 1519 and began operations by two symbolic acts: the burning of the ships which had brought him from Cuba, and the ceremonious founding of a municipality. To the magistrates of the 'town' of Vera Cruz Cortés resigned the commission he had received in Cuba; from them, as representatives of the Spanish Crown in Mexico, he received a new commission, and having thus legalised as best he could his assumption of an independent command, he led his army up the rugged climb from the steamy jungles of Vera Cruz to the high plateau of central Mexico. The outlying towns of the plateau, after some fighting, agreed to help him with food, with porters, and with fighting men; and by playing adroitly upon the superstitions of Montezuma, the Aztec war-chief, Cortés effected the peaceful entry of his army into Tenochtitlán, the capital city, built upon islands in the lake of Mexico. His peaceful occupation was short-lived; the zeal of the Spaniards in destroying heathen temples caused a rising in which Montezuma was killed, and Cortés had to fight his way out of the city along the causeways by night, losing in that one night a third of his men and most of his baggage. The auxiliary tribes remained loyal to the Spanish alliance, however, and Cortés was reinforced by another expedition from Cuba. He had boats built for fighting on the lake, and laid formal siege to the city, systematically looting and destroying it building by building as he advanced towards the centre, until in 1521 the surviving Aztecs surrendered. In the beautiful Spanish city which Cortés began to build on the site, there is hardly a trace of the former Indian buildings: the place was built over as completely as the Roman cities of Europe.

Cortés showed genius, not only in holding his own men together, but in securing at least the passive loyalty of the conquered Indians. He worked so wisely that there was never afterwards any serious trouble with the natives of the plateau region. His imitators in Central and South America were less fortunate or less adroit. The Maya territories in Central America were subdued with great brutality by Cortés' lieutenants. The Inca Empire, with its centre at Cuzco on the high plateau of the Peruvian Andes, was not discovered by Spaniards until 1530, after eight years of exploration, by land from Cartagena, by sea from Panama. The conquest of Peru was organised by a syndicate whose principal member was an obscure adventurer named Francisco Pizarro. Pizarro entered Peru with a smaller following even than that of Cortés. He was fortunate in finding a usurper on the Inca throne. In imitation of Cortés he contrived to seize the person of this reigning chief, Atahualpa, whom he afterwards executed. Like Cortés, also, Pizarro organised his conquests by founding municipalities with due legal pomp. Like Cortés, he sent his lieutenants exploring, south into Chile, and north to Quito and New Granada. But though he had all Cortés' generalship, Pizarro had little of the diplomacy and charm which Cortés displayed. His appointment as governor of the best part of the Inca dominions provoked fierce personal quarrels and eventually civil war among the conquerors. Francisco Pizarro, his brother Gonzalo, his partner and rival Almagro, and hundreds of their followers were killed. Their factions raged intermittently for nearly twenty years, and peace was restored with great difficulty by the intervention of the home government.

Naturally the surviving Indian rulers tried to turn the situation to their own advantage; but too late. Only in southern Chile did Indians arms prevail against the Spaniards. A major rebellion in western Mexico was crushed by the first viceroy, Antonio de Mendoza, in 1542. By 1550 all the chief centres of settled population in tropical America were in Spanish hands—but not in the hands of the great *conquistadores*. Private commanders like Cortés, Pizarro, Belalcázar and Nuño de Guzman, who depended for their power upon their personal following, if they escaped the knives of their rivals, were displaced by royal nominees. Exporation and conquests went on in frontier regions, in northern Mexico and east of the Andes; and in the fifteen-sixties a well-planned, ably-led, and almost bloodless conquest added the Philippines to the Spanish empire. In most parts of the Americas, however, the great age of the *conquistadores* ended when the principal settled areas were secure. Forests and empty prairies were not to their taste. Cortés spent his last years in bored and litigious retirement. There was little left for him to conquer.

(ii) *The theory of empire*

The Spanish conquest in America was a genuine crusade, appealing alike to the missionary's zeal for souls and the soldier's desire for military glory and for plunder. Unlike earlier crusades, however, it brought in its train an immense task of imperial government. The *conquistadores* had gone to America at their own expense, endured great hardships, risked their lives and fortunes—such as they were— without help from the Spanish state. Most of them looked forward to a pensioned retirement; some living in Spain upon the proceeds of their plunder, but many more living in the Indies upon the labour and the tribute of the conquered races, as the Incas and the Aztecs had done before them. Left to themselves, they would probably have settled in loose communities, employing the feudal forms which already were anachronisms in Spain, exploiting the Indians as the needs of the moment dictated, and according verbal homage but little else to the Spanish Crown. Many of the rebel leaders in Peru—in particular, Gonzalo Pizarro—contemplated just such a society, extravagantly loyal in sentiment but in practice virtually independent.

The rulers of Spain never for a moment thought of allowing such a state of affairs to persist. In the late fifteenth and early sixteenth centuries the Crown, with considerable bloodshed and expense, had successfully cut the claws of the great feudal houses, of the knightly orders and of the privileged local corporations. A growing royal absolutism could not tolerate the emergence of a new feudal aristocracy overseas. At the same time royal government was by no means a lawless or unbridled absolutism. The Church and the legal profession were its honoured partners and its most useful servants. The conquest of America touched not only the royal authority, but the royal conscience and the tradition of royal justice.

Discussion of the nature and duties of kingship, in both legal and theological terms, was a commonplace in sixteenth-century Spain. It was an age of vigorous and outspoken political thought, thought which was, for the most part, resolutely opposed to despotism and which placed the law of God and the laws and customs of free peoples above the will of kings. The conquest of a great and semi-barbarous empire obviously presented a difficult problem to the apologists for constitutional kingship. They all admitted—no Catholic could deny—that the bulls issued by Alexander VI in 1493 had given to the Spanish Crown the duty and the sole right of converting the American natives to the Christian faith. If the Indians resisted the preaching of the Gospel, they might lawfully be subdued by force of arms. The duty of civilising a barbarous people and the fact that the Spaniards were the first Europeans to discover America were valid, though secondary, reasons for the conquest. But if the Indians should be reduced by a just conquest, what legal and political rights remained to them? Should their rulers be deposed—if indeed they had legitimate rulers? Should they be 'converted' by force? Might they be enslaved, or deprived of land or property? Were they to be subject to Spanish courts of law, civil and ecclesiastical? What claims had the Spanish settler upon the tribute and labour of the Indians?

Spanish writers differed profoundly in their answers to these questions, and the main ground of difference was the nature of the Indians themselves. The colonists naturally emphasised the apparent idleness of people accustomed to subsistence farming, and the treacherous resentment of a conquered race. They claimed unfettered local lordship based on forced labour and maintained, not without some plausibility, that a paternal feudalism would best serve the interests of the Indians themselves. Many missionaries, on the other hand—in particular the famous Dominican preacher Las Casas— insisted on the purely spiritual nature of the Spanish enterprise. Las Casas's theory of empire rested upon the belief that the Indians, equally with the Spaniards, were the natural subjects of the Spanish Crown, and enjoyed from the moment of entering into the Spanish obedience all the guarantees of liberty and justice provided by the laws of Castille. He maintained that they were capable intellectually of discharging the duties of Spanish subjects and of receiving the faith. He contemplated an ideal empire in which the Indians would live under their own headmen but subject to the authority of bene- volent royal officials who would instruct them in European customs and persuade them to abandon barbarous practices. The Church would proceed peacefully with its work of conversion and spiritual ministration. If other Europeans, as private persons, were allowed to reside in the Indies, they would live apart from the Indians and support themselves by their own labour.

Las Casas was no mere theorist, but a devoted missionary who had himself pacified a large and savage tract of country in Central America. In Spain he was a powerful and respected personality. He represented, of course, an extreme view. The opposite view, that of the colonists, also had its defenders, notably Juan Ginés de Sepúl- veda, the distinguished scholar and humanist and friend of Erasmus, one of the ablest apologists of European imperialism. Between Sepúlveda and Las Casas, and between the schools and the interests which they represented, there was fierce and acrimonious debate. The importance of such controversies lay in the public interest which they aroused, and in their effect on royal policy. Spanish methods of government, as distinct from methods of conquest, were cautious, legalistic, slow, above all conscientious. They were influenced both by reports of practical experience and by considerations of abstract right. By the middle of the sixteenth century there emerged from the dust of controversy an official policy and an official theory of empire which, despite constant vacillations in matters of detail, were main- tained with very fair consistency for over two hundred years.

The Indies were kingdoms of the Crown of Castille, separate from the kingdoms of Spain, and administered through a separate royal council. The Indians were held to be subjects of the Crown, not of the Spanish state or of any individual Spaniards. They were free men, and might not be enslaved unless taken in armed rebellion. Their land and property were their own, and might not be taken from them. Their headmen were to be confirmed in office and employed as minor officials. They were to be subject to Spanish courts of law, and might sue Spaniards and be sued by them; but their own laws were to be respected except where they were clearly barbarous or repugnant to the Spanish laws of the Indies.

The Indians were, of course, to be converted to Christianity as soon as possible and were to be admitted to all the sacraments of the Church. Their conversion was to be free and not forced, and their lapses into heresy were to be dealt with by the ordinary jurisdiction of the bishops, not by the Inquisition.

To meet the claims of the colonists, the Crown granted to deserving conquerors and settlers the right to draw the assessed tributes of specified villages, by way of pension. These grants of *encomienda* involved no jurisdiction or territorial lordship; nor, after the middle of the century, forced labour. They did involve, for the *encomendero*, the obligation of military service and the duty of paying the salaries of the parish clergy. Forced labour was permitted—was indeed found to be indispensable; but under the *mita* or *repartimiento* system, the compulsion was applied by public, not private authority, and official wage-rates were laid down for labour so recruited.

Of course, the decrees enjoining this policy were often obstructed and sometimes openly defied; but that does not detract from the merits of the policy, as a product of sixteenth-century thought and experience. The enforcement of the policy, moreover, though incomplete, was by no means as incompetent as the enemies of Spain pretended.

(iii) *Soldiers, missionaries and lawyers*

The Spaniards who went to the New World were not settlers seeking an empty land, but soldiers, missionaries, administrators—a ruling class. They sought not to displace the native population, but to organise it, educate it, and live by its labour. They took over as a going concern the systems of tribute collection formerly organised by the dominant tribes in Mexico and Peru. Within a few years they created a number of deeply-rooted vested interests, which made the enforcement of a uniform official policy extremely difficult.

The most powerful group of interests was naturally that represented by the 'old conquerors' and their descendants. They formed a quarrelsome and disorderly society, whose good behaviour had to be bought with *encomiendas,* grants of land, and minor salaried offices. The one attempt made by the Crown to give legislative force to the proposals of Las Casas and to abolish the *encomienda,* in the 'new laws' of 1542, caused an armed revolt of the settlers of Peru, in which the viceroy was killed. The 'new laws' had to be amended; and the settlers constantly pressed for further concessions, in particular for the right to turn their *encomiendas* from terminable grants into entailed estates. There were never enough *encomiendas* or offices to go round, and almost from the beginning a 'poor white' class made its appearance, living among the Indians and giving endless trouble to the missionaries. Many settlers, rich and poor, took Indian wives, and so added a *mestizo* class to an already complex society. These people of mixed blood came in time to outnumber both pure Indians and pure Spaniards; and many of the Latin American peoples today are predominantly *mestizo.*

The Spanish settlers found their chief organs of expression in the town-councils, powerful and jealous of their privileges in the Indies as in Spain. There was nothing democratic about these bodies; they were local oligarchies. Councillors in the early days were appointed by military commanders or provincial governors, but in the second half of the sixteenth century the practice grew whereby they purchased their offices from the Crown for life. The councils elected municipal magistrates, and exercised wide administrative powers, not only within the town areas, but over considerable tracts of surrounding country. They corresponded directly with the Crown and were always determined upholders of local Spanish interests. They rarely displayed much constructive vigour, however. They were neither responsible, nor in any exact sense representative institutions; and in the seventeenth century, as the power of the *corregidores* increased and the sale of offices became more nearly universal, the councils sank into decline.

The Spanish conquest, however, was a spiritual as well as a military conquest, and the principal local opposition to the rule of swordsmen came from the soldiers of the Church—the friars of the missionary Orders. All three Orders, but especially the Franciscans, in the early days sent picked men to the Indies, and the conversion they sought to achieve was more than a mere outward conformity. The friars taught and preached, as soon as they were able, in the Indian languages. They established mission communities and made the mission Church the centre of the lives of many thousands of

Indians. They made at least a beginning in the provision of both primary and secondary religious and literary education for the Indians—an ambitious undertaking designed, ultimately, to prepare selected Indians for the priesthood. It is true that this last undertaking was, in the main, a failure. The Church in the Indies never produced a numerous native priesthood, and its spiritual strength and hold upon its converts ultimately suffered as a consequence. The reasons for that failure are too complex for analysis here; what is certain, is that the policy of the Orders in the sixteenth century interfered with the lord-and-vassal relation which the settlers sought to establish with the Indians. The difference in attitude was not merely one of humanitarian sentiment; for the *encomienda* and *repartimiento* were not inherently cruel institutions, though they led to many abuses. The important differences were legal and spiritual.

On the whole, the Crown endorsed the views of the missionary Orders, but dared not enforce them in full. The friars also differed among themselves, and they, too, could be rebellious and impatient of control; not, of course, to the extent of armed revolt, but in many lesser acts of indiscipline. They challenged the power of the Crown indirectly on many occasions, by flouting the authority of the bishops whom the Crown appointed.

The differences among Spaniards were reflected by differences among the Indians themselves. For the most part the Indians showed a surprising docility and resignation. Their acquiescent nature, under the shock of conquest, often sank into apathetic melancholy, broken only by religious festivals and their accompanying drunken orgies. In many provinces their numbers declined catastrophically as a result of the introduction of unfamiliar diseases, especially smallpox. In New Spain, disastrous epidemics occurred in 1521, 1545, and 1575-6. Among the settled peoples, the survivors tended to lose the material and spiritual culture of their ancestors, without fully acquiring that of the Spanish conquerors. They became strangers in their own land. Many tribes, however, remained unsubdued and dangerous throughout the colonial period, and even among the settled peoples wide differences persisted. Some Indian chiefs received *encomiendas* or became great landowners. Many others, if official reports are to be believed, willingly exploited their own people on behalf of the Spanish colonists. From the beginning, a considerable class of skilled workmen, household servants, and the like, threw in their lot with the Spanish community. In many parts of the Indies the old village life soon began to disintegrate, though not without protest. The Crown repeatedly insisted that Indian complaints should be freely heard, not only by the courts, but by the administrative authorities. The government even retained salaried advocates to present Indian pleas.

The royal insistence that all parties should have a hearing helps to explain one of the leading characteristics of Spanish colonial government—the great power and prestige of the professional judiciary. Ten *audiencias*—courts of appeal—were established in the Indies in the sixteenth century. The *audiencia* judges were always school-trained lawyers and always peninsular Spaniards. They were the only branch of the colonial service whom the Crown really trusted. Professional lawyers were the ideal agents of centralised government. They had no excessive family pride and no ambition, as a rule, for military glory. Their training gave them a deep respect for authority and a habit of careful attention to detail, while it discouraged any tendency towards rash or unauthorised action. Judges, moreover, representing the jurisdiction of the monarch, preserved a certain impersonality which helped them to control *conquistadores* who would have resented the authority of one of their own caste.

Every province had its governor and the governors of the two greatest provinces—Mexico and Peru—enjoyed the title and dignity of viceroys. Some of these governors were churchmen or lawyers; more were aristocratic soldiers; but under the suspicious Hapsburg kings, soldiers without armies. They were never trusted with the powers and temptations of independent command. Even a great administrator like Francisco de Toledo received inadequate support from home, and small thanks from Philip II for thirteen years of empire-building in Peru. Most viceroys served for much shorter terms, and all were carefully watched by their *audiencias*. The *audiencias* were much more than courts of appeal. They were cabinet councils empowered to advise the viceroys and governors in all administrative matters, to report on their conduct, and to hear appeals against their decisions. A viceroy might over-ride his *audiencia* temporarily, but on appeal to Spain the judges were likely to be upheld; for the Council of the Indies was itself a predominantly legal body, to which colonial judges might hope to be promoted in due course of seniority.

This cumbrous system of checks and balances might make for impartiality and respect for law—respect, at least, for the forms of law. It certainly did not make for administrative efficiency or speed of action. All important decisions, and many unimportant ones, were made in Spain. In the Indies, there was no decision which could not be reversed and no jurisdiction which could not be inhibited. Appeals and counter-appeals might hold up essential action for

years, until the occasion for it were forgotten. 'Obey but not enforce' became the administrative watchword of an empire whose
legislation and basic policy were, in many respects, models of en-
lightenment for their time.

(iv) *Atlantic trade and the silver fleets*

The characteristic occupation of the New World Spaniard was
stock-farming. It was an occupation peculiarly well suited to the
temperament of the *conquistadores*, an open-air life covering great
areas of country, offering considerable excitement, calling for great
skill in horsemanship and periodic outbursts of great energy, but
for the most part requiring no steady or sustained effort. In Spain,
the owners of flocks and herds were favoured socially and economically at the expense of the arable farmer; grazing rights tended
to override all other kinds of land rights. A similar situation soon
arose in the temperate parts of Spanish America, where the work
of arable farming was left mainly in the hands of the Indians. Horses,
cattle and sheep were imported in great numbers and multiplied
rapidly. As in all the economic activities of the Spaniards in the New
World, the methods used were slovenly and wasteful. Leather commanded a high price in Europe in those turbulent times; for an
ox-hide jerkin would turn a knife-thrust. Often the beasts were
slaughtered for their hides alone, the carcases being left to rot on
the ground. Nevertheless, the industry prospered. Great estates grew
round the ranch-houses, where the Spanish ranchers lived in patri-
archal state, surrounded by their poorer Spanish and *mestizo* dependants and their Indian *peones*.

In the tropical coast-lands, where cattle could not thrive, the principal Spanish product was sugar, which had been introduced into
the West Indies by Columbus and into Mexico by Cortés. Sugar
was a crop which lent itself to large-scale production, since fairly
elaborate equipment was needed for crushing the cane, extracting
and refining the syrup, and crystallising the final product. Sugar
plantations were started by many Spaniards, particularly near the
Caribbean and Gulf coasts. There was a steady demand for sugar—
then an expensive luxury—in Europe, and the industry prospered
reasonably in spite of wasteful methods and government interference. Both sugar and tobacco—a crop of great economic importance
in the seventeenth century—were largely produced by slave labour,
African Negroes being imported for the purpose. Since Negroes
were the subjects of barbarous African kings and not of the king of

Spain, there was no legal and little, if any, humanitarian objection to their purchase as slaves. They had to be obtained through Portuguese middlemen, and were extremely expensive in the Indies.

The animal and vegetable products of the Indies were almost insignificant to many Spaniards in comparison with the mineral products—the precious metals. Gold and silver mining in the early days of the conquest was a simple affair of prospecting and washing in likely streams; but about the middle of the sixteenth century, immensely productive silver veins were discovered at Zacatecas and Guanajuato in Mexico and Potosí in what is now Bolivia. Various forms of crude mass-production quickly took the place of the primitive washing process, and extensive plant—extensive for those days—was set up for extracting the silver from the ore, usually by a mercury amalgamation process. These developments produced lawless and exciting silver rushes, and special courts were hastily set up in the mining camps to register claims and settle disputes. Probably some Spaniards worked small claims by hand; but the typical silver miner was a capitalist and an employer of native labour, skilled and unskilled, on a fairly large scale.

The Crown claimed a share, usually one-fifth, of all metal produced. This was the income which aroused the envy and suspicion of all the other monarchs in Europe. In actual fact in most years it was probably not much more than ten or fifteen per cent of the total revenue of the Spanish Crown, and was pledged to German bankers long before it left America. The constant import of silver had disastrous effects on prices and on the economic structure of Spain as a whole—effects which contemporaries attributed to almost any cause but the right one. The economic theories of the time treated bullion as the most important and most valuable product of the Indies; the government sought by all possible means to encourage gold and silver mining, and to enforce payment of the bullion tax. A considerable body of officials was employed to weigh, test and stamp the silver ingots as they issued from the mines and to take out the royal share. Still further officials at the ports watched for attempts to smuggle unstamped silver. About the middle of the sixteenth century, a convoy system was devised for protecting the bullion cargoes on the Atlantic crossing. From 1564 two armed fleets were dispatched from Spain every year, one to Mexico and the Gulf ports, the other to the isthmus of Panama. Both fleets wintered in America and reassembled at Havana the following Spring for the return voyage. Each fleet consisted of from twenty to sixty sail, usually escorted by from two to six warships. It was forbidden for any ship to cross the Atlantic except in one of these convoys, unless special licence had been granted. The sailings were sufficiently regular for privateers to lie in wait for them, and one or two ships were lost almost every year. The whole plan illustrated Philip II's excessive confidence in the power of combination and weight, and his inability to see the value of manœuvring and speed—the very mistake which led to the Armada disaster of 1588. Still, on the whole the convoys served their purpose; they maintained regular sailings for a century-and-a-half, and only three times during that period was a whole fleet intercepted and defeated, once by the English and twice by the Dutch. The cost of the convoys was borne by a heavy and complicated series of duties on all goods carried from or to America; so the safety of the fleets was dearly bought, and the whole arrangement added greatly both to the delays in obtaining goods in the colonies, and to the price of the goods when they eventually arrived.

The trade to the colonies was a monopoly throughout most of the sixteenth and seventeenth centuries. The monopolist was not the Crown (as in Portugal), but the *consulado*—the merchant guild—of Seville, with its subsidiary organisation at Cadiz. By an elaborate series of fictions, merchant houses all over Spain became members by proxy of the Seville guild, consigning their cargoes in the name of resident Seville merchants. Even foreign commercial firms, German, English and Flemish, adopted this device, so that the genuine members of the guild performed a vast commission business which came to overshadow their own legitimate trade. Seville was the bottleneck of the Indies trade; a bottleneck still further narrowed by the licensing regulations of the royal House of Trade—licensing of emigrants, to prevent the emigration of Jews and heretics; licensing of ships, to ensure their sea-worthiness; of navigators, to ensure their competence. Some commodities might only be exported with special licence—firearms and Negro slaves, for instance. This regulation is understandable, since the Crown was always afraid of the possibility of a slave mutiny; but the whole system constituted a formidable obstacle to trade.

Apart from monopoly and regulation, there was a rigidity in the economic structure of Spain as a whole, which made a rapid expansion of export trade extremely difficult. Among the causes of this rigidity were the contempt widely felt for humdrum employment; the decline of handicrafts and agriculture, due to the Moorish wars and the expulsions of Jews and Moriscos; the privileges accorded to pastoral farming and the consequent damage to arable interests; the large proportion of people in unproductive occupations, especially the Church; heavy taxation and constant European war. Furthermore, the most flourishing commercial centres of

Spain, in Cataluña and Aragon, were committed to their Mediterranean connections, and had no great interest in entering the Indies trade.

The whole of the Indies was an eager market for cloth, weapons, tools and hardware of all sorts, books, paper, wine, oil and slaves. Spanish producers could not, or would not, export these goods in sufficient quantities or at competitive prices. The Indies trade therefore was a standing temptation, not only to pirates and privateers, but to slavers, smugglers and illicit traders of all nations.

5

FISHERMEN, EXPLORERS AND SLAVERS

(i) *The Atlantic fisheries*

The most spectacular achievements of the great age of discovery were incidents in the search for spices or precious metals; but these were not the only oversea products in high demand in Europe. Territories which produced neither came to be recognised as having a certain value of their own, and as being worth the trouble of exploring. Of all the articles of trade in fifteenth- and sixteenth-century Europe, fish was probably the most important. Monasteries and great men kept their own fish-ponds; but for most people, dried or salted fish was a vital food in the winter and on fast days throughout the year. Sea fishing, consequently, was a major industry; and the gradual failure of the Baltic herring fishery, for many years monopolised by the ships of the German Hanse, set fishermen of all nations searching the coastal waters of Europe and Iceland and venturing far out into the Atlantic.

Respect for the maritime strength of Spain and Portugal, rather than regard for papal bulls, kept the ships of other nations away from the discovered sources of species and precious metals. The north Atlantic, unfrequented by Spaniards or Portuguese, was another matter, and Henry VII felt himself at liberty to send John Cabot exploring there, despite rumbles of protest from Spain. Cabot reported that the sea off Newfoundland was teeming with great fish; but the first people to profit by this discovery were, once again, the Portuguese. One of Cabot's ship's company, according to a credible tradition, had been a Portuguese, one Fernándes, nicknamed 'the Labrador'—the farmer; and it was he who gave his name, first to Greenland, and then to the territory now called Labrador. Fernándes returned home and reported what he had seen. His reports were promptly followed up by the brothers Corte-Real, Portuguese resident in the Azores who made a series of voyages under royal commission to discover lands in the north-west within the Portuguese demarcation. Unlike Cabot, the Corte-Reals had no hope of finding spices, but they appreciated the value of Newfoundland as a source of timber for masts and spars, and they claimed the whole coast for Portugal. Labrador was generally thought at the time to be on the Portuguese side of the Tordesillas line, and it was so marked on the Cantino map of 1502. The coast was too barren to tempt either Spaniards or Portuguese to settle, but the Portuguese from the beginning of the sixteenth century began to exploit the fisheries of the Newfoundland Banks. Within a few years, cod-fish was coming into Portugal in large enough quantities to make an import tax on it worth while. The Portuguese thus forestalled both French and English, and remained always stout competitors. Many Portuguese fishermen in later years settled in New England, and their descendants may be met with in Province Town today.

The French were not far behind. A Norman ship brought a party of Indians, with the canoe in which they had been taken, to Rouen in 1509; and at least by that date both Normans and Bretons were fishing regularly on the Banks. Records of early English fishing trips are lacking; but the Cabots, father and son, were well known in Bristol, and the fishermen of the west-country ports were not slow to take advantage of their discoveries.

As the number of ships on the Banks increased, the nature of the trade changed, from the immediate sale of 'green' fish to the marketing, at longer intervals, of much larger quantities of 'dry' fish. The fishermen set up temporary shelters ashore during the summer months in order to dry and repair nets and smoke and salt the catch. No attention was paid to the territorial claims of Portugal; for there were no forts and no naval patrols. The beaches of the Newfoundland coast became the regular seasonal camp-sites of a tough and independent cosmopolitan fishing community.

The development of the North Atlantic fisheries had effects of far-reaching significance, both in Europe itself and in the story of European expansion. Obviously the import of great quantities of cod was in itself a significant economic event, in a continent where many people lived near starvation level for part of every year. The seasonal fishing camps, also, became centres for barter with the natives, so that the trade in furs grew up as a profitable sideline of the fishery. A natural desire to increase the effective length of the fishing and fur-trading season gave rise to plans, like those of Sir Humphrey

Gilbert in the later sixteenth century, to replace the seasonal camps by permanent settlements in Newfoundland and other parts of North America. These plans, it is true, did not emanate as a rule from the fishing community. Skippers of fishing craft were not long-term planners; their business was to make a full catch during the summer months, and get back home with it before the autumn gales. Most of them were bitterly opposed to any scheme for planting colonies in North America, whose inhabitants might compete with seasonal fishermen by fishing for a greater part of the year; but although the leaders of the fishing community were not interested in exploration for its own sake, fishermen often signed on for exploring voyages. Perhaps the most important result of recourse to the Banks was the increase in the numbers of ships and men fitted for long and hazardous ocean passages. A whole series of Tudor enactments referred to the fisheries as a nursery of ships and seamen, and the legislators spoke no more than the truth. The ships which sought the northern passages and opened the trade with Russia; the expeditions which began the settlement of North America; the English and Dutch fleets which defeated the navies of Spain, were largely manned by sailors trained in the hard school of the Banks fishery.

(ii) *The search for a northern passage*

The maritime states of northern Europe were by no means satisfied with the knowledge that their fishermen were reaping a rich harvest from the sea. Throughout the sixteenth century the demand for spices and other oriental goods remained as urgent as ever, and prices were as high, or higher; though now the profits were going to the Portuguese shippers and to the middlemen at Antwerp, which had become the chief European spice market. English, French and Dutch still hankered after a direct route to the 'Spicerie'. Magellan's Strait was too hazardous, the Cape route too well-guarded by the Portuguese. The great rivers which seemed to offer hope of passages to the Pacific were one by one explored and found hopeless: the Río de la Plata by Solís and Sebastian Cabot, the Hudson (perhaps) by Verrazano, the St Lawrence by Cartier. There remained only the possibility of sailing round, or threading through, the northern extremities of America or Europe.

To navigators who habitually used a globe, it seemed obvious that there must be a more direct route to the East across the Arctic, than round the Cape of Good Hope; and so, of course, there is, except that it is only possible for aircraft. Most sixteenth-century maps show the Arctic as open sea, with large but widely separated islands. Little was then known of the vast extent of the northern ice-cap. Seamen argued that the Tropics had proved passable, contrary to all expectations; why not the Arctic? A considerable number of northern voyages were planned in England, and financed either by special syndicates, or by the trading companies which were being formed about the middle of the sixteenth century. In particular the 'Company of merchant adventurers for discovery of regions, dominions, islands and places unknown' had as its first Master old Sebastian Cabot, who had been pilot-major of Spain, and who after his disappointments in the north-west and in the Río de la Plata, was determined to investigate in the north-east.

In 1553, the Company dispatched a fleet of three ships under Sir Hugh Willoughby with the express intention of sailing to China by way of a north-east passage. The names of the ships are worth mentioning for their gallant though misplaced optimism. They were the *Bona Speranza*, the *Bona Confidenza* and the *Edward Bonaventura*. Off the Lofoten Islands the ships were separated by a storm. Two of them, including Willoughby's flagship, put into an inlet somewhere near North Cape. There they were soon frozen in and all their company died of cold and starvation. The *Edward*, however, commanded by the senior navigator, Richard Chancellor, entered the White Sea and reached Archangel. Here Chancellor learned for the first time of the power and wealth of the Russian emperor, and after long haggling with the local people, he and some of his officers set off on an astonishing journey in horse-drawn sleighs, in winter, from Archangel to Moscow.

Russia at that time was almost completely isolated from other civilised countries. It was hemmed in by nomad peoples to the south and east; it was allowed no intercourse with militant Catholic Poland to the west, and its only seaboard, to the north, was ice-bound for much of every year. Within this isolation, Ivan the Terrible and his predecessor had achieved a considerable measure of order and national unity throughout Great Russia. Ivan's only contact with Europe was through the ships of the north German Hanse. As it happened, relations with the Hanse towns had been broken off shortly before Chancellor's arrival for a variety of political reasons, and Moscow was suffering from the resulting shortage of imported manufactured goods—woollen cloth and above all, arms of all kinds. England produced these things and was also a steady market for furs, hemp and tallow, which Russia produced. For these reasons the English adventurers were doubly welcome, as civilised strangers and as merchants. Chancellor, fortunately, was a competent diplomat as well as a fine seaman. He was received with a terrifying royal hospitality. His visit led to an opening of trade and a long series of diplomatic exchanges, extending even to tentative suggestions of alliance and royal marriage.

The results of these exchanges were not entirely happy. Ivan's interest in England was not only commercial, but diplomatic, military and social. Elizabeth's interest in Russia was commercial only. The intercourse between the two countries was marked by cross-purposes and misunderstandings, as it has been almost constantly ever since. That was not the fault of Chancellor or of Antony Jenkinson, his successor. Their personal relations with Ivan were excellent always. Chancellor was a visionary of unusual power and in one of his reports he wrote an appreciation of the Russians which is worth quoting:

'If they knew their strength,' he wrote, 'no man were able to make match with them, nor they that dwell near them should have any rest of them, but I think it is not God's will; for I may compare them to a young horse that knoweth not his strength, whom a little child ruleth and guideth with a bridle, for all his great strength; for if he did, neither child nor man could rule him.'

Commerce between Russia and England never amounted to much in the sixteenth century, despite its fair beginning. The Muscovy Company, formed to exploit it, was comparatively short-lived. The journey to Russia was too long and difficult and the risks were too great. Russia was not to appear as a permanent figure on the European stage until the time of Peter the Great; but this does not detract from Richard Chancellor's achievement. His voyage was one of the greatest English voyages of discovery, though it contributed little to a solution of the problem of the north-east passage. Subsequently attempts to find the passage were made by servants of the Muscovy Company, and later in the century by a series of Dutch explorers, the most prominent of whom was William Barents. The Dutch continued the search until 1624, but their voyages resulted only in the collection of information about Spitzbergen, Novaya Zemlya, and the north coast of Russia. This knowledge was of use, not indeed to spice-merchants, but to whaling skippers. Both the English Muscovy Company and various Dutch concerns were interested in whaling, and the steady development of the Arctic whale fishery in the late sixteenth and early seventeenth centuries was largely inspired by reports brought home by seekers for the north-east passage.

The north-west passage had even more weighty support, from

both ancient and modern geographers, than the north-east. Sir Humphrey Gilbert's persuasive *Discourse* on the subject gives an impressive list of authorities. The actual search, which began with Frobisher's first voyage in 1576, was another story of heroism, of failure in its main purpose and of successful results in unexpected directions. Frobisher made three voyages; he was diverted from his search for a passage by the discovery and shipment to England of quantities of worthless 'gold ore'. His work was continued from 1585 by John Davis, who sought the passage in the sea which separates Greenland from the North American archipelago; and after the turn of the century by Hudson, Bylot and Baffin. All these men are commemorated in the names of capes, bays and islands in Arctic America. They were all Englishmen; for the north-west passage, alone among early exploring projects, was a mainly English enterprise. Apart from the increase of geographical knowledge, the chief practical result of their work was the discovery, in Hudson's Strait and Bay, of a back door to the richest fur-producing region in the world, a region which otherwise would have been monopolised by the French. In the later seventeenth century this vast and lonely Arctic bay was to carry an adventurous and profitable trade, and to become a hotly contested international waterway.

(iii) *The interlopers in America*

The weakness of the Spanish commercial system in America was for nearly three centuries a constant factor in the European economic situation. Spain could not supply more than a fraction of the requirements of its colonies. While Spaniards at home sought to maintain high prices and a rigid monopoly, Spaniards in the colonies wanted abundant supplies at low prices and were willing to trade with foreigners in order to obtain them. There was an easy and ready market in the Indies for any ship-owner who could under-sell the regular merchants of Seville and who was ready to risk possible trouble with the colonial authorities. The first foreigner who systematically exploited this market was Sir John Hawkins, the founder of the English slave trade.

During Mary's reign and the early years of Elizabeth, the English were in a strong position to make a bid for a peaceful trade with America. Relations between England and Spain were relatively friendly. The Spanish government was even capable of using the offer of a share in the Indies trade as a political bargaining-counter. At worst, an English merchant would not be taken for a pirate on sight, as a Frenchman would have been. Of the two commodities, most in demand in the Indies—cloth and Negro slaves—the English produced the first and could purchase the second in West Africa at the risk of a brush with the Portuguese authorities—a risk which they minded less and less as the century wore on. Hawkins had at least a reasonable hope of securing some sort of Spanish trading licence; he was no smuggler; he was prepared to pay all legal dues, and in return for a licence he declared himself willing and able to help in clearing the Spanish Main of its chronic plague of pirates, and in particular to attack and destroy a troublesome settlement of French Huguenots, which had recently been established on the coast of Florida, near the Florida channel.

Hawkins, however, was not disposed to apply directly to the Spanish court and to endure all the delays and prevarications which such an application would have involved. He proposed to embark on the Indies trade at once, and to prove his good intentions by his good works. In 1562 he set out on his first slaving voyage—a modest venture of three small ships, but brilliantly planned and executed. His first call was at Teneriffe in the Canaries; here, through the good offices of a business acquaintance, he signed on a Spanish pilot, and sent word to the buyers in Hispaniola that he would be arriving later with a cargo of slaves. At Sierra Leone, his next call, he procured three hundred Negroes, some captured on the coast and some purchased from Portuguese factors, who subsequently complained to Queen Elizabeth that Hawkins had used force to compel them to sell. With this cargo, Hawkins sailed across the Atlantic to Hispaniola. Here, after much negotiation, he obtained from the local authorities permission—which they had no power to grant—to sell his slaves. He paid the official customs duty and licence fees, and made a very handsome profit. He even secured local testimonials to the effect that he had behaved correctly and engaged in peaceful trade; so that everybody appeared satisfied.

Hawkins accepted payment for his slaves in the form of hides and sugar, both valuable commodities in Europe. The cargo was so bulky that he had to charter two extra ships in Hispaniola in order to get the stuff home. Rather surprisingly, he despatched one of these ships to Spain, consigning its cargo to a business friend in Seville. The cargo was a small one; probably Hawkins's object was to test the Spanish reaction to his voyage, and to prove that he was a licensed trader and no pirate. The cargo was confiscated as soon as it reached Seville and Hawkins's attempts to recover it, through the Spanish ambassador in London, were unavailing.

Hawkins at once began to make preparations for a second voyage on a much bigger scale; and this time the Queen and several of her Privy Council were shareholders, though naturally their participation was not made public. Hawkins took his cargo on this occasion to the mainland ports of Venezuela and the Isthmus. He followed the same procedure as before, sold his slaves with an occasional show of mock force, received similar testimonials of good behaviour, and again made a large profit, much of the return cargo being silver. When he reached England, however, there were two pieces of bad news awaiting him. One was that the able and ruthless Admiral Menéndez had gone to the Indies with a frigate squadron, had destroyed the French settlement in Florida, and was busy clearing out the nests of pirates from the Antilles. Menéndez' success clearly reduced the value of Hawkins's offer of service to Philip II. The other news was that the Spanish government had started prosecutions against those colonial officials who had dealt with Hawkins, and had instructed the Spanish ambassador in London to make a vigorous protest against the contraband trade in slaves. England was at peace with Spain and Elizabeth intended to remain at peace; she sternly forbade Hawkins to go to the West Indies again.

Hawkins observed the letter but not the spirit of the Queen's orders; he sent one of his captains, a man named Lovell, in command of the next expedition. Lovell had great difficulty in selling his slaves, for the local authorities were becoming thoroughly frightened. In 1567, Hawkins persuaded the Queen to change her mind, and allow him to command one last voyage in person. That voyage was a disaster. The little fleet was trapped in the harbour of San Juan de Ulúa by the annual convoy, arriving several weeks before its expected date with the new viceroy of New Spain on board. For the first time in his life Hawkins had to deal, not with Spanish colonials who were willing to evade the law in their own interests, but with high Spanish officials whose careers depended on maintaining the law. To the viceroy, Hawkins was a heretic pirate with whom no faith need be kept. Entering the harbour under cover of a pretended truce, the Spanish fleet opened fire, and sank or captured three of Hawkins's five ships. The other two, one commanded by Hawkins himself, and one by his cousin, Francis Drake, eventually reached England in a sinking condition, with their company dying of starvation, in January, 1569.

This fight meant the collapse of Hawkins's great plan for trade. In Hawkins's absence, the Spanish Netherlands had rebelled against their masters. Two years later Queen Elizabeth was excommunicated by the Pope and her subjects absolved from their allegiance, and two years after that, hundreds of French Protestants were mur-

dered on Saint Bartholomew's Eve. War between Catholic and Protestant interests was clearly only a matter of time.

For the next thirty years Protestant sea-captains visited the
Spanish Indies as pirates and privateers rather than as peaceful,
though illicit, traders. Nevertheless, the demand in Europe for
American silver, sugar, leather and tobacco, and the demand in
America for slaves and manufactured goods, continued to rise. Once
Hawkins had shown the way, the English, French and Dutch mercantile communities would not rest content to buy American products in small quantities at high prices from grasping middlemen in
Seville. Illicit trading never entirely ceased, and with the return of
peace, merchants of all nations resorted to the Caribbean, with considerable success. In 1611 Sir Thomas Roe, cruising off the Guiana
coast, noted in Trinidad harbour twenty-four merchant ships, English, Dutch and Flemish, 'freighting smoke'—that is, loading tobacco.
There is no reason to suppose that the Spanish silver which continued to come to England was all the result of piracy. Throughout the seventeenth century, a share, or better still, a monopoly of
Spanish American trade was one of the chief prizes for which the
maritime peoples of Europe contended.

(iv) *The privateers*

The battle of San Juan de Ulúa was an important episode in that
steady deterioration of Anglo-Spanish relations, which culminated
in the Armada action. Actual war broke out in 1585, but for fifteen
years before that the Caribbean was the scene of intermittent privateering war. Drake himself went back to the West Indies in 1571 and
again in 1572, on both occasions as a privateer rather than as a merchant. Queen Elizabeth was coming to sympathise more and more
with the policy of Drake and his friends, and while officially disa-
vowing their activities she supported them, though with misgivings,
in secret.

Piracy and privateering were, of course, no novelty off the Spanish
Main, but hitherto the privateers had been mainly French. During
the long period of intermittent war from the accession of Charles
V to the treaty of Câteau-Cambrésis in 1559, French letters of
marque had been issued freely to ship-masters who wished to
plunder Spanish shipping. During part of this period there was a
treaty of alliance between France and Portugal, which meant that
licensed privateers were required to leave Portuguese ships alone, but
had the use of the Azores as a base for attacks on Spanish shipping.

The damage they did was considerable. In 1537—their most successful year—they took nine ships out of a total sailing of twenty odd. In 1556, Captain François le Clerc, whom the Spaniards called *Pie de Palo*—'a seafaring man with one leg'—with ten warships sacked the town of Havana itself and scuttled all the shipping in the harbour. In 1562, Jean Ribault, with the secret connivance of Coligny and in despite of Câteau-Cambrésis, planted his ill-fated colony in Florida as an advanced base.

The Spaniards, of course, had their answer to these depredations. Shortly after the middle of the century their convoy system began to take shape. A little later, frigate squadrons were stationed at Havana to patrol the two main sea lanes, from Havana to Vera Cruz and from Havana to Nombre de Dios on the Caribbean shore of the Isthmus. The organisation of these patrols was entrusted to Pedro Menéndez, one of the great sea commanders of the century. Menéndez began the building of the great fortifications of Havana. He constructed dockyards in the Indies capable of building and refitting light warships. He achieved remarkable improvements in the discipline and armament of the convoys, and in the course of his career he captured more than fifty corsair ships. He shared with Drake and Nelson the strategic genius which treats all seas as one. His long-term remedy for the menace of English privateering was a bold and brilliant plan for striking at the privateers' home ports from a base in the Scilly Isles. But Menéndez had no time left him to create the admiralty organisation which his plans required. He died in 1574, in one of those swift epidemics which so often ravaged the fleets of that day.

Menéndez' death was a loss which Spain could ill afford. Religious bitterness, in the fifteen-seventies, was adding another motive to the existing reasons for privateering. Corsairs were taking to the sea in greater numbers and with greater boldness even than in Le Clerc's day; and that other naval genius, Francis Drake, was being loosed upon the Indies in independent command of voyages of reprisal.

Drake's first reprisal voyage of 1571 was a reconnaissance in which he obtained a few small prizes and a good deal of information about the Isthmus of Panama; and in which he established contact with French corsair captains and with communities of maroons, the offspring of untamed Indians and runaway Negro slaves. With these allies he embarked in the following year on an ambitious plan for intercepting a Peruvian treasure consignment at its most vulnerable point, on the long haul by mule-train across the Isthmus to the Caribbean port of Nombre de Dios. Drake's preparations were in

startling contrast to those favoured by Hawkins and other more conservative commanders. The ships, although probably supplied by
Hawkins, were small enough to operate close inshore, and to escape
by using their sweeps if pursued by warships in the fluky airs of the
Caribbean. Drake's own men numbered only seventy odd. Even with
his allies, he had too few men to hold Nombre de Dios itself, but he
ambushed and captured a mule-train laden with treasure on the
road, and got most of the booty back to his ships, and home to
England, in the summer of 1573. This brilliant raid established
Drake's reputation as a privateer captain.

When Drake returned, he found that the scare of immediate war
with Spain had blown over. Several other privateers made raiding
trips between 1573 and 1576; but Drake's next employment in 1577,
was in an ostensibly peaceful mission, to follow Magellan's route to
the Pacific and to establish trade relations with the rulers of treasure
or spice-producing countries there, including possibly the Moluccas.
This project of the south-west passage was thus complementary to
the expedition led by Frobisher to the north-west. The events of
Drake's amazing voyage are well-known: the passage of the Strait
in sixteen days—a record for the century; the raids on the Spanish
ports of the Pacific coast (for which Drake may have had secret and
verbal permission from the Queen); the capture of the *Cacafuego*
with her load of Peruvian silver; the exploration of the North
American coast, in search, it may be, of the mouth of the northern
passage. From refitting in his remote Californian anchorage, Drake
crossed the Pacific in the north-east trades, reached the Moluccas,
concluded an informal treaty with the Sultan of Ternate—then at
war with the Portuguese—bought several tons of cloves, and sailed
home by the Portuguese route round the Cape. He was the first
English captain to sail either the Pacific or the Indian Ocean, and
of course the first to circumnavigate the globe. His voyage, more
than any previous one, showed the vulnerability of the coast of
Spanish America and put a stop to any possibility of further Spanish
expansion across the Pacific.

The rest of Drake's naval career was occupied in real and admitted
war with Spain, and the same is true of most of his contemporary
friends and imitators. In this war, American matters became sub-
merged in the general fighting; but almost every general treaty
concluded both during and after the war had some bearing on
colonisation and trade. In 1596, at the treaty of The Hague, France
under Henry of Navarre, England and the Netherlands formed an
alliance against Spain which looked strong enough to dismember the
Spanish empire. It failed to fulfil its promise, however; the French

made their peace separately in the treaty of Vervins in 1598. Henry
IV, according to later accounts, tried to secure a share of the American trade in this treaty, but his attempts—if indeed any were made
—failed. The treaty makes no mention of them. In 1604, the pacific
James I having succeeded Elizabeth, England also made a separate
peace—the treaty of London. In the negotiations for this treaty a
new and important principle was enunciated: James declared himself willing to recognise Spanish monopolistic claims to all territory
effectively occupied by Spain, but admitted no Spanish rights in unoccupied parts of America. In the truce of Antwerp of 1609, which
ended for a time the war between the Netherlands and Spain, and
which recognised the Dutch as an independent nation, the same principle was embodied in a formal clause. This principle of effective
occupation is now a familiar rule of international law relating to
discovery and annexation; as enunciated at the beginning of the
seventeenth century, it was a warning that the English and Dutch
intended to colonise in North America whether the Spaniards liked
it or not.

6

THE STRUGGLE FOR EASTERN TRADE

(i) *The Muslim East*

In 1580, Philip II succeeded to the throne of Portugal after a short war to vindicate his claim. One of the clauses in the treaty which recognised him as king was a promise that all offices and opportunities of profit in the Portuguese Indies should be left to Portuguese subjects. On the whole Philip kept his promise; but the ultimate responsibility for the administration and defence of the empire in the East fell upon the Spanish Crown, and from the Portuguese point of view the results of the union were disastrous. Spain in the late sixteenth century was engaged in a bitter struggle against Protestant England, against France and against Philip's own rebellious subjects in the Netherlands. The trade and the possessions of Portugal in the East, as well as those of Spain in America, became the legitimate prey of the sea-faring enemies of Spain. At the same time, the political situation in the East itself grew steadily less favourable to the Portuguese.

The balance of power in India had changed since Albuquerque's day. When the Portuguese took Goa, the power of the Muslim sultanates of central India had been counter-balanced by that of Vijayanagar, the formidable and fabulously wealthy Hindu kingdom in the south, whose territories stretched from the Kistna to Cape Comorin. In the frequent quarrels between this Hindu kingdom and its Muslim neighbours, the interests of the Portuguese would have been best served by Hindu victory or by stalemate; but Portuguese efforts to this end were feeble and half-hearted. In 1520, a handful of Portuguese musketeers served in the army of the Hindu King Krishna Raya against the Sultan of Bijapur. More important, the

Portuguese supplied Krishna Raya with large numbers of imported horses every year for the use of the Vijayanagar cavalry. Krishna Raya on one occasion offered Albuquerque a considerable sum of money for a monopoly of the purchase of horses in order to keep them out of the hands of the Muslim sultans. Albuquerque, with an eye to present profit, refused the offer; but as events turned out, he would have done well to accept. After the death of Krishna Raya in 1529, the Hindu kingdom entered upon a steady decline. Finally it was defeated and dismembered by a league of the central Indian Muslim sultanates, Bijapur, Ahmadnagar, Golconda and Bidar. The battle of Talikot in 1565 marked the end of the kingdom of Vijayanagar as a potent political force and placed the Muslim princes in undisputed command of most of south and central India.

One of the inevitable results of this Muslim victory was an agreement among the sultans to drive the Portuguese out of Goa and the other coastal fortresses. The attack on Goa began in 1569; its defence against overwhelming odds was one of the most brilliant feats in Portuguese history, and entitled the viceroy Luis de Ataide to rank among the great soldiers of the world. Command of the sea—the only route by which reinforcements might come—saved the Portuguese garrisons from annihilation; but only after two years of fierce fighting did the sultans abandon their attempt.

Meanwhile in north India even more momentous events had been taking place. At the time when the Portuguese arrived in India, the sultanate of Delhi, under an Afghan dynasty, had been passing through a period of disorder and decline and the Hindu Rajput princes had recovered something of their old power; but in 1524 the supremacy of Islam was restored by a fresh invasion. The invader was Babur 'the Tiger', a Baghtai Turk by race, descended on his father's side from Timur the Lame and on his mother's from Chinghiz Khan. Babur entered India, to recapture the old possessions of his family, with a small army of central Asian horsemen and —significant and decisive innovation—a battery of Turkish artillery. He possessed himself of the Delhi kingdom in two major battles. At Panipat in 1526, he defeated and drove out the Afghan Sultan; and at Kanua in 1527 he broke up the Rajput confederation. Babur was the founder or re-founder of the Delhi empire of the house of Timur, miscalled by Europeans the Mughal empire—the most powerful state in India, ruled by a series of able and vigorous princes. The Mughal emperors were not, therefore, native to India, any more than the Portuguese. They were of central Asian origin; their mother-tongue was Turki; the official and literary language of their court was Persian. With one notable exception they were orthodox and often persecuting Muslims.

Since the Mughals were exclusively land warriors and the Portuguese were fighters by sea, the first contacts between them were indirect. They arose from the attempts of Babur's successor, Humayun, to extend his authority over the independent Muslim sultanates of north India, in particular the maritime state of Gujerat which, at the time, was in a state of chronic disorder and civil war. The ruler of Gujerat, threatened with invasion by the Mughal, asked for Portuguese help, and in 1535, the Portuguese, in return for a promise of military assistance (a promise they never fulfilled), received a site for a fortress and warehouse at Diu, and other territorial concessions. Shortly afterwards, Humayun abandoned his enterprise; but the Portuguese remained at Diu and beat off all the attempts of the Sultan of Gujerat to dislodge them. Diu became, after Goa, one of the most important bases of Portuguese power in India.

Humayun's successor on the Mughal throne was Akbar, the greatest of his line and one of the most remarkable sovereigns of any time. So vigorous a ruler clearly would not tolerate a source of constant disorder in Gujerat. The Portuguese, appreciating by this time the power which the Mughals wielded, refused to be enticed into any alliance against Akbar. To the Emperor, it must have been a source of great vexation to find important ports like Diu and Bassein in the hands of alien merchants; but he saw at once that the Portuguese could not be dislodged without the use of a fleet, which the Mughals never possessed. When, therefore, Akbar reduced Gujerat to obedience in 1572–3, he entered into courteous relations with the Portuguese and left their warehouses alone. In 1578 a Portuguese ambassador was accredited to Akbar's court, and in 1580, the first Jesuit mission visited the Mughal capital. Akbar was characteristically interested in all religions, and like Kublai Khan in the thirteenth century, was disposed to give Christianity a fair hearing. In this, however, he stood alone, and the Portuguese could not hope for a like tolerance after his death.

In the late sixteenth century, then, the Portuguese maintained, by gallantry and good fortune, a profitable but still precarious foothold on the coast of India. They had no land empire worth mentioning, and no friends; for India had fallen more and more into the hands of Muslim rulers who regarded the Portuguese at best with guarded tolerance, at worst with bigoted hatred. The Portuguese position depended entirely on their command of the sea; and the appearance in the Indian Ocean of an enemy who could defeat them at sea might well prove fatal to their power. The Turks had several times tried and failed; in the end it was a European enemy who succeeded.

In the East Indies as in India, the spread of Islam was continuous. The old Hindu empire of Majapahit, which once covered most of the archipelago, had long been breaking up, and in the sixteenth century it disappeared, to be succeeded by a complex of Muslim sultanates. In Sumatra, Atjeh grew to prominence in answer to the Portuguese challenge at Malacca. Two powerful sultanates, Bantam and Mataram, emerged in Java; and since the Strait of Malacca was now partly closed to Muslim traffic, they developed an alternative trade route through the Sunda Strait. Only in the island of Bali, Hindu religion and culture held their own. In the Moluccas, a succession of able and vigorous sultans of Ternate gave the Portuguese governors endless anxiety, and in the fifteen-seventies the Portuguese fort at Ternate was besieged for five years. In these circumstances, the union with Spain was almost welcome, bringing as it did Spanish support from the newly-occupied bases in the Philippines. In the East Indies, as in India, the Portuguese position, though tenaciously held, was precarious. A powerful maritime rival might at any time accomplish its destruction.

(ii) *The decline of Portuguese power*

The troubles of the Portuguese in the East arose not only from external pressure, but from internal weaknesses. The decline in the efficiency of their commerce and administration towards the end of the sixteenth century can be attributed to three principal causes: their small numbers; their practice of racial intermarriage; and their uncompromising religious policy.

The first two causes of weakness are closely connected. The Portuguese were a small nation. Very few of them settled permanently in the East, and hardly any women. There was no strong colour prejudice, and inevitably those white men who spent any number of years out east took Indian wives. This practice was encouraged by Albuquerque and most of his successors. Even in Portugal itself at this time an admixture of African blood was being introduced from the Guinea coast. In India the white strain tended to become absorbed and to disappear altogether. The principal danger to Portuguese power lay in the difficulty of manning ships and fortresses. Under the fearful conditions of mortality on board the ships of the time in the Tropics, a constant stream of recruits was necessary on the spot, and only Indians or half-castes were usually available. The west coast of India bred some fine deep-water sailors, but most of them, the Gujeratis especially, were hostile to Portuguese power.

The Indian seamen available for manning Portuguese ships were not the best.

Only the necessity of manning the ships with such Indians and half-castes can account for the decline in seamanship in the Portuguese fleets as the sixteenth century progressed. Decline in manning efficiency was accompanied by growing carelessness in buoyage and pilotage. There were numerous complaints in Portuguese reports in the early seventeenth century that interloping English and Dutch shipmasters knew the estuaries of the Malabar coast more thoroughly than did the Portuguese who had been using them for years; and that they took far more trouble to train the general run of their officers in navigation. Commercial motives, also, compelled the Portuguese to use larger ships for the Indian trade; but improvements in design failed to keep pace with increases in size. In the late sixteenth century the initiative in nautical development had passed from Portugal to the Netherlands and England. The combined effect of all these changes is shown vividly in the figures of ship losses for the century. In the eighty odd years from Vasco da Gama's first voyage to the union of the Spanish and Portuguese crowns, 620 ships left Portugal for India. Of these, 256 remained in the East, 325 returned safely to Portugal and 39 were lost. In the next forty odd years—from 1580 to 1612—186 ships sailed, 29 remained in the East, 100 returned safely, 57 were lost. In the first period, therefore, 93 per cent of the ships which sailed from Portugal reached their destination safely; in the second period only 69 per cent found harbour. This decline in the efficiency of the fleets struck at the very root of Portuguese power in the East—the command of the sea lanes from Asia to Europe.

The failure of the Portuguese to maintain their early dominance at sea was not offset by any trustworthy system of alliances with the native powers on land. Such alliances were made difficult, if not impossible, by the religious policy of the government, especially after the union with Spain. When Vasco da Gama first reached Calicut and was asked by its ruler what he had come to seek, he is said to have answered tersely 'Christians and spices'. There were, of course, considerable numbers of Nestorian Christians in South India. Da Gama's followers even confused Hindus with Christians; at least they were prepared to regard all who were not Muslims as potential Christians. Since the crusading zeal of da Gama, Albuquerque and their like took the form of a commercial and religious war against Islam, and since when they arrived the struggle between Hindu and Muslim for the control of south India was still undecided, it is surprising that the Portuguese did not ally themselves with the Hindu community. It was their good fortune to make their first landings in Hindu territory; had they landed in Gujerat their reception might have been very different. In fact, however, they lacked the necessary knowledge of the Indian situation as a whole, and their first friendly feeling soon hardened into religious hostility. They quarrelled with the Zamorin of Calicut; they alienated the Zamorin's rival, the Raja of Cochin, by unnecessarily hard bargaining over prices; they made no serious attempt to establish relations with the suzerain Hindu state, the empire of Vijayanagar.

Even in dealing with the Hindu inhabitants of the places where they settled, the Portuguese from the first showed a singular lack of understanding. The caste system was a mystery to them. Even Albuquerque, usually punctilious in such matters, on one occasion asked the Raja of Cochin to have some men of low caste, who had assisted the Portuguese, raised to a higher caste, and took offence at the Raja's refusal. That such matters were beyond the Raja's power seems never to have occurred to him. Brahmin notions of ceremonial purification caused constant trouble. Portuguese admirals attributed the refusal of Brahmins to dine on board their ships to the fear of poison, and were quick to take offence at the ceremonial cleansing which had to be undergone by Brahmins who visited Portuguese ships. Even the native Nestorians—the 'St. Thomas's Christians'—received no encouragement from the Portuguese; and indeed after the arrival of the Jesuits were treated more harshly, as heretics, than were Hindus.

Albuquerque and his immediate successors on the whole left Hindu religious customs alone, except for attempts to suppress the rite of *sati*. But missionaries followed upon the heels of the crusaders; the relations of the Portuguese commanders to the Church inevitably changed as ecclesiastics came to form a larger and larger proportion of the white inhabitants; especially since the Jesuits, shortly after the foundation of their Order, selected Goa as their second headquarters outside Rome. In 1540 came the royal order for the destruction of all Hindu temples in Goa. The early intermittent methods of the friars, mainly Franciscan, who arrived with the annual fleets, blossomed into a native church under the apostolic teaching of St Francis Xavier, who reached India in 1542. Independently of the apostolate of St Francis, there emerged a system of civil regulations designed to exclude non-Christians from all public office. In 1560 the Inquisition arrived to deal with heretics and apostates. The accession of a Spanish zealot to the Portuguese throne in 1580 increased the official pressure upon the native religions. The Synod of Diamper in 1599 denounced Nestorius and his heresies and for a time extinguished the Indian Nestorian Church as an organised community in Portuguese territory.

The fervent apostolic mission of St Francis and his followers was one of the outstanding achievements of the Counter-Reformation Church. To this day, not only in what is now Portuguese India, but throughout Ceylon and in many of the Malabar towns, there are large numbers of Catholic Christians who bear Portuguese baptismal names and who are conscious enough of their separate communal existence to wear a distinguishing dress, but they have never been more than a fraction of the whole population. The Muslims were hardly touched by Christian preaching. Both Hindus and Nestorians were too numerous, too civilised and too deeply attached to their own ways to be converted *en masse* by a handful of European friars, however devoted. Moreover, the Christian attitude towards other religions was alien to the normal tolerance of the Hindus. The majority of conversions were made among persons of low caste seeking to escape from the pressure of the caste system. The result of the zeal of crown and missionaries was often to make the Portuguese hated, not only as pirates, but as religious persecutors. By one of the unexpected coincidences of history, in the same year 1599 in which the Synod of Diamper condemned the ancient church of Malabar, the London merchants met in Founders' Hall to establish an East India Company.

(iii) *The Companies*

Drake's voyage of circumnavigation revealed to Europe that the Portuguese, so far from being masters of the East, were defending immensely long trade-routes and widely-scattered strongholds against a host of jealous enemies. Almost at the same time, the union of the Spanish and Portuguese crowns included Portugal in the hatred and fear with which the Protestant nations by now regarded Spain. Portugal was a potential enemy at home and a potential victim abroad. English politicians considered it dangerous that two such empires should be united under one king; and the outbreak of war removed the diplomatic obstacles to an open policy of dismemberment, or at least of intrusion and plunder.

Economic events pointed the same way. The revolt in the Low Countries interrupted the Dutch carrying trade between Portugal and Antwerp and made it difficult for the northern nations to obtain the oriental products they required. The ships of the English Levant Company, which had been bringing considerable quantities of East-

ern goods from the Syrian ports by virtue of a treaty with the Ottoman Sultan in 1579, now found that their passage through the Straits
of Gibraltar was disputed by Spanish and Portuguese men-of-war.
This throttling of trade was compensated to some extent by privateering successes, such as Drake's taking of the *San Felipe* off the
Azores in 1587 and Burrough's capture of the *Madre de Deos*
in 1592—both homeward-bound Portuguese Indiamen. But these
windfalls were a poor substitute for regular trade through Flanders;
and as the war dragged on it became clear that in order to obtain
spices the English and the Dutch would have to fetch them, sailing
to the Indies by the route which the Portuguese used rather than by
some doubtful and hazardous Arctic passage.

Queen Elizabeth first gave her consent to a direct intrusion in
the Indies trade in 1591. The expedition of Raymond and Lancaster
in that year was a costly experiment, since two of the three ships
were lost; the third reached Malaya and Ceylon and returned to
England, after many buffetings, with a cargo of pepper, but with
only twenty-five survivors. Tip-and-run voyages of this sort had
achieved considerable success in clandestine trade with the West
Indies; but they were inadequate to capture the trade of the East.
A permanent commercial organisation was needed, furnished with
adequate capital and adequate information.

Information was forthcoming, towards the end of the century, of
a more detailed sort than that supplied by the circumnavigators
Drake and Cavendish. An Englishman named Fitch had been sent
in 1583 on a land reconnaissance, similar to that undertaken by da
Covilhã a century before. Fitch bore letters from Queen Elizabeth
to the Emperor of China. He was captured by the Portuguese at
Hormuz and spent some time in captivity at Goa. Escaping from
there, he visited Akbar's court in northern India, found his way to
the Burmese coast and Malacca, and back by way of Bengal and
Cochin. He returned home in 1591 and set all London talking of
Portuguese misrule and the wealth of the Indies trade.

More important than Fitch was the Dutchman Jan Huyghen van
Linschoten, who had lived in India from 1583 to 1589 as a servant
of the Portuguese archbishop of Goa. Linschoten returned to Holland in 1592, and in 1595–6 he published an *Itinerario*—a geographical description of the world, including the author's personal
observations of the East, and a series of sailing directions for reaching America and India. This work became a best-seller in several
languages and supplied a direct impulse for the foundation of the
Dutch and English East India Companies. As the English translator
put it: 'I doo not doubt, but yet I doo most heartily pray . . . that

this poore Translation may worke in our English nation a further
desire and increase of honour over all Countreys of the Worlde' by
means of 'our Wodden Walles.'

Linschoten's sailing directions supplied exactly what the Dutch
needed. Dutch sailors were already sailing to the East in Portuguese
ships; but the yarns of deck-hands—even of officers—do not
amount to a reliable guide for navigators. Such a guide was now
available. The first Dutch fleet using Linschoten's sailing directions
sailed in 1595. The chief merchant of this expedition, Cornelis de
Houtman, was a ruffian who provoked quarrels almost everywhere
he went, and the trading results of the enterprise were disappointing.
As a reconnaissance in force, however, the voyage served its purpose.
Houtman had himself lived for some years in Lisbon; he probably
knew some of the weaknesses of the Portuguese position, and certainly exploited one of them by signing a commercial treaty with the
Sultan of Bantam, the Muslim prince whose fortresses commanded
the Sunda Strait.

Houtman's expedition was followed by a series of voyages
financed by various Dutch companies and syndicates. In the one
year 1598, five fleets sailed, comprising twenty-two ships. Nine attempted the western route by Magellan's Strait; of these only one
reached the East Indies. Thirteen took the Cape route, and of
these, twelve arrived safely in the East. Admiral van Neck, who
commanded one of the 1598 fleets, reached the Moluccas, traded in
Ternate, Banda and Amboina and concluded commercial treaties
with the rulers of those islands, all of whom were on bad terms with
the Portuguese. The Dutch were well received almost everywhere.
Unlike the Portuguese they did not in these early voyages mix their
commerce with piracy or proselytising, and their fleets were equipped for competitive trading. Their greater ability as sailors and the
better construction of their ships enabled them to carry spices to
Europe far more cheaply than the Portuguese could do, and their
trade goods—helmets, armour, weapons, glass, velvet and German
toys—were carefully chosen for their market. Such trading adversaries could be kept out of the Indies only by overwhelming naval
force; and Portugal, dragged at the heels of Spain into a major war in
Europe, was in no position to apply such force. The first actual battle
between Dutch and Portuguese ships, in the roadstead of Bantam
in 1601, was a decisive victory for the Dutch, against superior numbers but inferior manœuvring and armament.

The competition between Dutch and Portuguese, and still more
between different Dutch companies, encouraged the local sultans and
their subjects to raise their prices, tolls and harbour dues against

Europeans. Partly to prevent this raising of prices and to create monopolistic buying conditions, partly to strengthen the hands of Dutch commanders in treating with native rulers and fighting the Portuguese, the States-General decided in 1602 to amalgamate the various companies trading in the East into one great national concern, the Dutch East India Company. This company received a monopoly—as far as the Dutch were concerned—of trade between the Cape and Magellan's Strait. It might make war or peace, seize foreign ships, establish colonies, construct forts and coin money. In return, the States-General exacted customs dues and retained the rights of financial and general supervision of the company's affairs. The chief shareholders were merchants of Amsterdam and of other subscribing states and towns, though the opportunity of investment was open to all Dutchmen. The governing body, both in the persons of its directors and in its public policy, was closely connected with the States-General. Immediately upon its establishment it began to build forts in the East, to appoint governors, and to make treaties with native princes in the name of the *Stadhouder*; for Eastern notions of government made it necessary for the staunchly republican Dutch to represent their union as a monarchy in order to command respect.

England had an East India Company already. Its charter had been approved by the Queen at the end of 1600. Its first fleet sailed to the East in 1601, under Sir James Lancaster, the surviving captain of the 1591 voyage. This venture was highly successful; Lancaster bought a full cargo of pepper in Bantam, and captured a Portuguese carrack on his way. The English company, however, was a much more modest affair than the Dutch. Its subscribed capital was much smaller, and was, moreover, purely temporary, for the group of private merchants who organised the enterprise intended to undertake single voyages at three-year intervals, winding up their accounts and distributing both capital and profit after each voyage. Like most overseas trading companies operating from England at the time, the company held a chartered monopoly; but that was the full extent of government help which it expected or received. The Crown expected vigorous and profitable action in return for the grant of a charter; but the quicksand policy of the early Stuarts gave no guarantee that the grant would not be rescinded, or damaged by conflicting concessions to favourites. The whole matter was of less moment to the English government than to the Dutch; for the English did not live by trade—they were still primarily a nation of farmers. Though the company began with fair prospects, therefore, its trade

to the East Indies could survive only so long as relations with the
Dutch remained friendly, and so long as the Dutch would tolerate
English ships visiting what they came to regard as their preserves.

(iv) The Dutch East Indies

While their war with Spain continued, the Dutch accepted English
competition in the East Indies, and the two nations traded side by
side in reasonable amity. During this period the English East India
Company made five voyages with varying success. A number of
ships were lost, but one voyage—the third—showed a profit of 230
per cent. In 1609 the company secured a new charter, which granted
a perpetual monopoly in place of the original term of fifteen years,
and contained a stringent clause against the intrusion of interlopers.
So strengthened, the company dispatched annual fleets in 1610, 1611
and 1612, all of which showed a profit; and in 1612 it took a step
forward in organisation by inviting subscriptions for a terminable
joint stock over a period of years instead of for single voyages. From
1601 to 1612 the company had sent out a total of twenty-six large
ships and, discounting for the delay in winding up voyages, had
made an average profit of about 20 per cent. While the English
company worked patiently to secure this relatively modest profit,
the Dutch with their greater capital resources, with more powerful
home support and with five times more ships, fastened their grip
upon key points in the archipelago. Everywhere they appeared as
the deliverers of the local princes from the Portuguese, and everywhere they secured their position by treaties, first of commerce, then
of alliance, and finally of protectorate.

In 1609, the truce of Antwerp brought fighting to an end between
Spain and the independent Netherlands. England had made a separate peace in 1604, and any gratitude the Netherlanders may have
felt for help received while Queen Elizabeth lived was forgotten in
resentment against her successor's conciliatory attitude towards
Spain. In the Indies, trade rivalry became, after 1609, a bitter fight
for monopoly. From that year the Dutch began to assert exclusive
claims in the Moluccas. In 1611, the first governor-general of the
Dutch East Indies arrived at Bantam, and a general movement began to squeeze out the English from the island trade. All the resources
of propaganda were used to discredit the English with the natives;
their ships were stayed and their goods seized upon technicalities;
they themselves were imprisoned for imagined disturbances. Their
only redress lay in litigation before courts set up by the Dutch

authorities and instructed to grant no redress. In desperation the English company sent out an armed fleet in 1618 to protect its factors and in 1619 there was sharp fighting. The company's ships could achieve little, however, against the odds they were facing; insistent appeals to the English government produced nothing more effective than diplomatic protests and compromise agreements with the States-General which were worth less than the paper they were written on. The power and the initiative remained with the Dutch empire-builders in the East.

Of these empire-builders the ablest and most celebrated was Jan Pieterszoon Coen, who was appointed governor-general in 1618. By that time the sultans of the archipelago were beginning to regret their early enthusiasm for Dutch alliances, and the naval and political position of the Dutch was still insecure. Coen was for the Dutch what Albuquerque had been for the Portuguese, and more. He founded the naval and administrative capital of the East Indies, Batavia in northern Java. He secured possession of key points throughout the Indies, turning a network of trading posts into a chain of strongholds and pointing the way to a solid and enduring colonial empire governed by Dutchmen. He showed his countrymen that the long-haul trade between Asia and Europe was a trifle compared with the great volume of inter-asiatic trade which the Dutch might—and eventually did—largely control; unlike the Portuguese, who had hardly touched this trade except by sporadic acts of piracy. He recognised, perforce, that Asiatics were better traders than Europeans, and so, like Albuquerque, based his policy ultimately upon force, though not upon religious war. He superseded the Portuguese in the East Indies and made it possible for his successors to expel them from Malacca (in 1641) and from Ceylon (in 1658). Finally, he and his officers completed the business of driving the English from the archipelago.

The last harassed little band of English factors and merchants at Amboina—by then become the most important district in the Spice Islands and firmly under Dutch control—were arrested by the Dutch authorities in 1623 on suspicion of a conspiracy against the colonial government. After a trial in which confessions were extracted by torture, the condemned, ten in number, with some Japanese servants, were executed. The Amboina executions caused a great stir in London; but the political situation in Europe required the English government to remain on good terms with the States-General, and apart from diplomatic protests, no effective action was taken. English trade was at an end in the Moluccas and—except for a forlorn little factory at Bantam—in the East Indies as a whole.

The main object of the English East India Company was thus abandoned.

For the rest of the seventeenth century the English company confined its activities to the less profitable trade with the mainland of India. From 1607 company's ships had been putting into Swally Roads, the deep-sea anchorage for Surat, the capital of Gujerat, and in 1612 the Mughal governor of Gujerat, after some hesitation, granted leave to the English to rent—but not to own—a warehouse at Surat. Sir Thomas Roe, sent as the accredited ambassador of James I to the Mughal court, further secured in 1616 a general permission for the English to reside at Surat and to trade with the interior. There was no question of fortification. This was not a treaty between equal sovereigns, but a favour granted by the Emperor to Roe as a petitioner. It might not have been granted, but for two naval encounters in Swally Roads in which Portuguese fleets were heavily defeated—by Captain Best in 1612, and by Captain Downton in 1615. The authorities at Delhi—exclusively land fighters as they were—conceived the idea of employing the English ships as a mercenary naval patrol, and in 1629 even issued letters of marque to the company's representatives at Surat. It was under the protection of a mighty Asiatic empire, therefore, that the English company entered the trade in Indian calicoes and muslins and embarked, haltingly at first, upon a career which was to make it the heir to the Mughal power.

7

THE ENGLISH PLANTATIONS

(i) *The theory of settlement*

James I's policy towards Spain was one of conciliation; in the negotiations leading to the treaty of London in 1604 he would not have insisted so strongly on the right to visit unoccupied territory unless his government had had some definite colonising project in mind. There was clearly no hope of inducing the Spanish government to countenance regular trade with the occupied parts of America; and in peace-time solid investors would be reluctant to finance smuggling and privateering ventures. The only solution seemed to be for the northern nations to seize and colonise empty territory in America and mine the silver, cut the timber and grow the sugar for themselves. There was no question, at this stage, of seizing territory actually occupied by Spain; no European nation felt strong enough to risk attempting that. On the contrary, it was thought desirable at first that new colonies should be situated well out of reach of Spaniards. Sir Walter Raleigh, one of the first Englishmen to interest himself seriously in the project, had proposed two different places. One was Guiana, the swampy no-man's-land between Spanish Venezuela and Portuguese Brazil—a most unsuitable place. The other suggestion was Virginia, and Raleigh himself made determined attempts to found an English colony there, but without permanent success. Virginia was generally considered to be the best unoccupied place for a European settlement on the Atlantic coast of North America, being recommended both by its soil and by its climate. There were counter-arguments, however, for planting colonies much farther north, as bases for the fishing industry. Sir Humphrey Gilbert, the chief Elizabethan champion of this policy,

was lost at sea before anything could be achieved. In the more prosperous days following the end of the Spanish war, the projects of
Raleigh and Gilbert were realised by their successors and many small
settlements, some French, some Dutch, but mostly English, were
established in a long string from Newfoundland to Barbados.

Like the Spaniards, the English in America sought to found permanent colonies where they could live, own land, and rear families
—not mere trading stations. In England, as in Spain, the problems
of colonisation were the subject of careful and detailed discussion,
but with different results. Psychological differences between the two
races, different circumstances in America, and a century of time
between the foundation of the two empires, together account for the
wide differences in theory. The English colonies were almost all
planted in places where there was either no native population, or
only a sparse and primitive one, numerous enough to be dangerous
but too wild to be employed as a labour force. This was a matter of
necessity, not of choice. The Spaniards had seized most of the territories where docile native labour existed. English promoters of
colonisation had therefore to transplant whole communities with a
complete labour force of Europeans. These men had somehow to be
induced to emigrate. The cost of their emigration had to be paid,
and their tools, seed and equipment provided from England by the
promoters. The risks, responsibility and expense were more than
a private individual could normally undertake, and colonisation was
usually, therefore, a joint-stock enterprise in which a considerable
number of people might invest their money without necessarily ad-
venturing their persons. In order to float such a company, with a
legal title to the soil and with authority to govern the settlers, a royal
charter was necessary, or at least desirable. The books and pamphlets
put out by English promoters of colonisation, therefore, were comparatively little concerned with theory, with the legal and religious
rights and wrongs of conquest and settlement. They were designed
to attract emigrants and investors and to solicit government approval
for particular enterprises.

Religion could not be left out of the argument, of course, in discussing any major enterprise in the seventeenth century. Like the
Spaniards, the English theorists appealed to religious feeling and
missionary zeal. Every colonising company in every European country in the seventeenth century claimed the spreading of the Gospel
as its leading motive. John Smith in Virginia told his followers
that: 'The gaining provinces addeth to the King's Crown; but the
reducing heathen people to civility and true religion bringeth honour
to the King of Heaven.' The Massachusetts Bay Company an-

nounced that 'as the propagating of the Gospel is the thing we do profess above all to be our aim in settling this plantation, we have been careful to make provision of godly ministers'. Even among the Puritans, however, there was far less active missionary fervour in England than in Spain, and the North American Indian was a less promising neophyte than his Mexican or Peruvian contemporary. Convention required the inclusion of religious arguments; the religious motive was always present, but usually subordinate.

Some English writers used political arguments, appealing to the current anti-Spanish feeling, which persisted long after the peace of 1604. One of the petitions of the Virginia Company suggested 'the inestimable advantage that would be gained to this State of England in case of war, both for the easy assaulting of the Spaniards' West Indies from those parts, and for the relieving and succouring of all ships and men-of-war that should go on reprisals'. Spain, however, was still a power to be respected. The early Stuarts were too cautious and too impecunious to attempt a large-scale attack on the Spanish West Indies, and the anti-Spanish argument was a minor factor in inducing the government to support colonisation in America.

There was an important social argument in favour of colonisation. The England of James I suffered from widespread unemployment and from a rapid growth in the size of the big towns, especially London. Contemporary economists, having no reliable statistics, concluded that the country as a whole was over-populated, and many of them looked to colonies as a vent for the surplus population. To quote one example among many—William Vaughan's *Golden Fleece*, an eccentric but shrewd economic and social allegory published in 1626:

'This main business,' wrote Vaughan, 'is to be promoted in regard of the general populousness of Great Britain, which is the chief cause that charity waxeth cold. Every man hath enough to do to shift for his own maintenance, so that the greatest part are driven to extremities, and many to get their living by other men's losses ; witness our extortioners, perjurers, pettifoggers at law, coney-catchers, thieves, cottagers, inmates, unnecessary ale-sellers, beggars, burners of hedges to the hindrance of husbandry and such like, which might perhaps prove profitable members in the New Found Land.'

The fear of over-population was temporary, without real foundation. It gave way in the second half of the century to the opposite fear, that colonial emigration would rob England of badly-needed

manpower; but the 'vent' theory of colonisation weighed power-
fully with statesmen in James I's day.

The most important arguments, however, were economic. The
colonies were to enrich the investors, and the realm in general, by
producing commodities which were in demand in Europe; to enrich
the Crown by means of customs duties; and to enrich the merchants
and manufacturers of England by serving as markets for English
products. This last argument lost some of its force as the sparseness
and poverty of the native population became better known; more
cogent was the claim that the colonies would be a source of supply.
The commodities chiefly sought fell into four main groups: the
precious metals, much the most important in contemporary economic thought; fish, a vital article of diet, much of which was imported into England by the Dutch; wine and other luxuries normally imported from Portugal and the Mediterranean; naval
stores. This last item was naturally of strategic as well as economic
importance. Ever since Englishmen began to use the sea, England
had been short of fir poles for masts, pitch for caulking seams and
hemp for cordage. Most of these things came from the Baltic and
access to them could be denied by whatever power controlled the
shores of the Sound. An alternative supply of naval stores was thus
a powerful attraction. Apart from strategic considerations, mercantilist opinion naturally welcomed the possibility of importing
from colonies instead of from foreign countries and of securing surplus products for re-export to Europe.

The most striking feature in all this economic discussion is its
optimism, its cheerful assumption that all America yielded precious
metals, that any warm country such as Virginia might be made to
grow vines and mulberry trees. The capital and the effort required
to exploit the wealth of America were greatly under-estimated, and
in most ways the reality of the American empire was to differ considerably from the mercantilist dream. Despite initial hardships,
however, enough capital and enough labour were found to establish
a number of modest but successful colonies in the first half of the
seventeenth century. These colonies fell roughly into three groups:
Virginia with its immediate neighbours and satellites; New England
with its little groups of emigrant nonconformist settlements; and
the West Indian Islands. In terms of their early economic development these groups can be labelled respectively as the tobacco colonies, the fish, fur and timber colonies, and the sugar colonies.

(ii) *The planting Companies*

The Virginia Company was incorporated in 1606 and began operations in that year, though its definite charter was not issued until 1609. This document was an adaptation of the familiar type of charter granted to joint-stock trading companies. The general government of the company was entrusted to the whole body of shareholders. A man could become a shareholder in two ways: the first, by investing money, by buying shares. A share was valued at £12 10s., which was the estimated cost of planting one settler. Alternatively, he could become a shareholder by investing his person, by emigrating to Virginia at his own expense with his family and servants. One body equalled one share. After an initial period of common labour, land was to be distributed among the shareholders, whether emigrant or not, in proportion to their investment. The emigrant shareholders became planters or free-farmers, paying only a small quit-rent to the company. They at first composed, and subsequently elected, the colonial assembly. This body, once the colony was firmly established, might make laws not repugnant to the laws of England, and voted colonial taxes; but it had no other lawful control over the governor and his executive council, who were appointed in the early days by the directors of the company in London. Virginia, therefore, and most subsequent English colonial foundations, had the germ of representative government, but not of responsible government.

The Virginia assembly represented an oligarchy—the freeholders. Below them in the social scale were the indented servants—men who emigrated at the expense of the company or of individual employers, binding themselves in return to work for a fixed term of years, hoping on the expiry of their indentures to set up for themselves as tenants or even free-holders. Most of the labourers and many of the artisans were men of this class; but the colony could never get enough labour, and soon the ranks of the indented servants began to be swelled by convicted felons whose death sentences had been commuted to life transportation, in order to people the colonies. Transportation meant, for practical purposes, slavery. White labour from this source was less unwelcome than might be supposed; for in those days of severe penalties a convicted felon was not necessarily a professional criminal in the modern sense. No clear line divided the felons from the indented servants, some of whom were themselves unwilling emigrants.

The directors, and investors generally, hoped to draw their dividends from quit-rents, from trading on their own account, and from duties levied on the trading of other merchants. They sent out volu-

minous instructions concerning the planting of profitable crops, the
working of mines, and the provision of naval stores. These instructions were never carried out. For the first few years the colonists were
hard put to it to feed, house and defend themselves, even with help
from England. More than half of them died within a few months of
their arrival. Probably all would have died, had it not been for the
inspiring leadership and the Indian connections of John Smith at the
beginning, and the character of the early governors, a series of
old-soldier martinets who by savage discipline kept their people to
clearing and ploughing instead of wandering about the woods hunting and searching for gold-mines.

The colony was saved from economic extinction and raised to
modest wealth by the cultivation of a single crop, tobacco. The art
of growing and curing tobacco had been learned from the Spaniards
in the course of voyages to Guiana. It might be supposed that the
authorities would welcome the production in Virginia of a commodity which otherwise had to be bought from Spain. Admittedly
Virginia leaf was then inferior in quality to that grown in the Spanish
Indies, but that was the kind of disadvantage which mercantilist
theorists expected the consumer to put up with. Smoking, however,
offended social and economic prejudices. It was considered not only
wasteful, but immoral, much as drug-taking is regarded today.
James I himself disliked the habit and wrote a pamphlet against
it—the *Counter-Blast to Tobacco*. The company sanctioned tobacco-
growing reluctantly, of sheer necessity; for tobacco supplied the
only means whereby the colonists could buy the manufactured goods
they needed. Virginia became a one-crop colony, subject to all the
distress caused by fluctuations of price, when, as inevitably happened, the English market became glutted. The Crown had no choice
but to acquiesce, and finally, in order to give the colonial producers
a steady market, it agreed to exclude foreign tobacco by means of a
high tariff and to prohibit the growing of tobacco in England, although this involved destroying a considerable acreage of the crop
in the west Midlands. The interests of English farmers and con-
sumers were to that extent sacrificed to those of the Virginian
planters.

Tobacco saved Virginia; it did not save the Virginia Company.
The company never paid a dividend, and by 1623 it was insolvent.
The worst feature of its insolvency was its inability to do anything
to help the settlers, and their distress was evident from the letters
which they sent to the Privy Council. Factious quarrels among the
directors made matters worse; and one faction, led by the Puritan
Sir Edwin Sandys, tried to drag the dispute into Parliament. James I

quickly put a stop to discussion, on grounds of prerogative; and in 1624 he himself began *quo warranto* proceedings against the company. As a result, the charter was revoked, and Virginia became the first, and for many years the only crown colony. This meant that the Crown appointed the governor and executive council; but James confirmed the right of the planters to elect their own assembly, and the right of the assembly to make laws and vote taxes. The structure of governor, council and assembly endured down to the war of Independence. The cost of royal administration was appropiately defrayed by an export duty on tobacco.

Meanwhile, in the disputed waters of the Caribbean, buccaneering, slave-running and illicit trade still went on, and the old fear of Spain was giving way to a familiarity which bred contempt. Within twenty years of the treaty of London, English, Dutch and French syndicates were forming plans for trading settlements in the Caribbean area. Their contempt for Spain and its satellite at that time, Portugal was not entirely justified. The Dutch, for instance, with a powerful and well-organised West India Company, tried persistently to settle in north-western Brazil; but the Portuguese settlers drove them out from everywhere except the little corner which became Dutch Guiana. The English Amazons Company of 1619 lasted only four years. The Guiana Company, a bigger concern, put up a longer struggle, but all its settlements were eventually destroyed by the Spaniards and in 1638 the company became bankrupt. These Guiana projects had important indirect results, however, for the dispossessed settlers, looking for alternative sites, lighted upon fertile islands in the Lesser Antilles. The Spaniards had left these islands alone, largely through dislike of the native Caribs, an intractable race whose war-like ferocity and cannibal habits had horrified the early discoverers. English landings on Dominica and St Lucia were beaten off by these Caribs; but St Kitts was successfully occupied by English and French settlers acting in collaboration, and most important of all, in 1624 the settlement of Barbados—until then uninhabited—was begun.

The financial backing for these undertakings came from a number of informal merchant syndicates, of which the most important were Warner and Associates, old Guiana men, and Courteen and Associates. Sir William Courteen was a London merchant with Dutch connections. These connections proved useful, for it was the Dutch planters in Brazil who supplied first the tobacco and then the sugar plants which were to be the basis of West Indian prosperity. The interests of the two firms overlapped, and in order to oust Courteen the Warner party secured the support of a prominent but impecu-

nious courtier, the Earl of Carlisle, who in 1627 obtained a patent
from Charles I creating him Lord Proprietor of the Caribbees. This
was the first appearance of a new type of English colonial organisation, the propriety. It was the application to America of a form of
grant long obsolete in England—a quasi-feudal grant of territory
and jurisdiction to a prominent nobleman. Obviously a peer could
obtain grants of this kind from the Stuart kings more easily than a
group of merchants; and it was perhaps thought more appropriate
that settlements in exposed positions should be made by feudal
grant in the old tradition of knight-service rather than by trading
companies.

The Carlisle grant led to constant quarrelling among the heirs
of the earl and the lessees of their rights; but in spite of political
uncertainty Barbados flourished. In the early years the colony produced mainly tobacco, cotton and various dyes, fustic, indigo
and so on, important in view of the persistent attempts in the English
cloth trade to change from the export of undyed cloth to that
of the finished article. In 1640, sugar planting was introduced,
mainly at the instigation of Dutch traders who had learned the
methods of cultivation and manufacture from the Portuguese in
Brazil. The Dutchmen sold to the Barbadians the equipment needed
for the crude processes of crushing, boiling and pot-crystallisation,
and taught them a little later the washing which turned brown sugar
into the much more valuable white. Sugar soon became the principal product. Its value per acre was three times that of tobacco in the
sixteen-forties and its price remained much steadier, for the European market seemed insatiable. Contemporary theory also approved
the cultivation of a crop which could not be grown in England and
which had been bought hitherto from foreign countries, chiefly from
Brazil through Portuguese or Spanish middlemen. Emigrants
flocked to Barbados, as planters or indented servants, and the island
received its share of transported felons. The considerable capital
expenditure required for sugar production, however, dictated the
division of the land into comparatively large plantations. These
estates employed mainly slave-labour. Many white small-holders,
and servants whose indentures had expired, moved to other colonies or took to buccaneering. The slave-owning planters remained,
and both they and the merchants who handled the sugar made large
fortunes. By the middle of the century the exports from Barbados to
England were considerably greater in value than those of Virginia
and very much greater than those of New England; and Barbados
was already known as 'the brightest jewel in His Majesty's
crown'. Except that the governor was appointed by the proprietor

and not by the Crown, the administration of the island was similar to that of Virginia.

The rapid development of the sugar islands had two important consequences in the realm of colonial policy. In the first place, there grew up on the sugar plantations an insatiable demand for labour. which together with the equally insistent demand in Spanish and Portuguese America stimulated the large-scale development of the transatlantic slave trade. The second consequence was a marked shift of opinion in England in favour of tropical colonies rather than temperate ones. Negro slaves were apparently cheaper than white indented servants, and actual deliveries of dyestuffs and sugar were better than vague promises of naval stores. While Virginia and New England had disappointed expectations as far as the home market was concerned, Barbados had greatly exceeded them. Under the Commonwealth and Protectorate, increased interest in the West Indies strengthened the arguments of anti-Spanish fanatics like the Earl of Warwick, in urging Cromwell to undertake the Western Design against the Spanish Indies in 1655; an undistinguished expedition whose only result was the capture of Jamaica.

The chief Spaniard-haters in England, for both religious and commercial reasons, were naturally the Puritans. They were also conspicuous colonisers. A company formed by prominent Puritans was incorporated in 1629 to settle Santa Catalina or Providence Island, in the heart of the Spanish Caribbean. The island was peopled by settlers from England and from Bermuda and in the early years both its planting and its seafaring activities showed considerable promise. Buccaneering soon outstripped planting as a source of profit, however, especially after 1631, when the company extended operations to Tortuga, off the coast of Hispaniola. Tortuga was frankly a buccaneering base and nothing else. In settling colonies of this kind so near the Spanish coasts, the company had attempted more than it could perform. In 1641, a Spanish fleet recaptured the islands and expelled the settlers; and the Providence Company came to an end. Tortuga fell eventually into the hands of the French and later became the base for the French conquest of Haiti. The permanent colonising successes of the English Puritans were achieved in a very different latitude.

(iii) *The Puritans*

The promoters of colonisation in the sixteen-twenties included an increasing number of people who had money to invest, who were interested in America, and who had an additional motive for wish-

ing to emigrate in person instead of remaining in England waiting
for dividends. This additional motive was usually dissatisfaction
with the religious and constitutional policy of the government, and
the persecution of Dissenters which accompanied it—persecution of
a mild sort as persecution went in those days, but still strong
enough to make godly Dissenters feel that the day of wrath was at
hand; as indeed it was. These dissatisfied people were the principal founders of New England.

A company or council for New England had been incorporated
at the same time as the Virginia Company; but New England had a
harsh, stony soil, heavily timbered, and a bitter winter climate. The
council failed to find either the men or the money to begin planting,
and by 1620 were willing to lease part of their grant to any who
would settle under their auspices. In that year the *Mayflower* arrived
in New England waters carrying her little band of Puritan emigrants
with their wives, dependants and indented servants. The Pilgrim
Fathers were quite humble folk, members of a dissenting congregation who some years before had emigrated to the Netherlands for
conscience' sake, and had then, thanks probably to Sir Edwin
Sandys's puritan sympathies, obtained permission to settle in the
northern part of the Virginia Company's territory. They sailed for
Virginia; but making their first landfall near Cape Cod, they decided to stay there and to found their settlement at New Plymouth.
The New England Council, when they heard of it, granted a lease
on easy terms, and the work of building up a settlement began.

The Pilgrim Fathers had to struggle not only against the wilder-
ness and the New England climate, but against a heavy burden of
debt, for they had emigrated on borrowed capital. They soon discovered that their only hope of being allowed to live their own life
as they wished was to buy out the investors' interest and to make
themselves economically independent. This they eventually succeeded in doing; but the effort involved many years of hard work
in grinding poverty, and for long the settlement remained small and
weak. Many of the settlers died in the first winter. Those who survived did so through their own amazing courage and patience, and
through the forbearance of the Dutch West India Company, which
was beginning to settle at the mouth of the Hudson and could have
wiped out the Plymouth colony if it had wished. The early difficulties of New Plymouth served as a warning to the Puritans in
England, that future settlements, to be sure of success, would have
to be undertaken by properly incorporated companies with adequate financial and social backing.

Not all the settlers in New England were Puritans. The fur-trader

Thomas Morton lived happily with a few companions, trading with the Indians and probably supplying them with rum. He wrote a delightful book, *The New English Canaan*, full of a woodsman's contempt for the town and village-bred Puritans. But in general, the initiative in New England remained with the Puritans. Their position in England was growing steadily worse. With the assumption of personal rule by Charles I, all hope of Presbyterianism in the Church, and all hope of parliamentary government in the State, seemed at an end. At the same time, the bitter and destructive war in Europe and a series of bad harvests at home made the economic outlook in England very uncertain. Many people of influence, wealth and Puritan sympathies, became willing not only to invest in colonisation, but to emigrate themselves. In 1629, a powerful syndicate consisting largely of prominent Puritans obtained a grant of land for settlement in New England, and incorporated themselves by royal charter as the Massachusetts Bay Company.

To outward appearance the new enterprise resembled the Virginian plan closely. Similar rules governed the rights of shareholders, planters and indented servants; but the charter had one significant peculiarity—it did not explicitly require the government of the company to remain in England. That the document passed the seals with this omission is in itself surprising. Puritan lawyers, it is true, were not above sharp practice where they considered the Lord's work to be involved, and they certainly exploited official ignorance of geography in obtaining a gross infringement of the rights of the New England Council; but neither inadvertence nor bribery seems adequate as an explanation. Whatever the means employed, a group of shrewd business men were in fact empowered by charter to retain property rights in England and the formal status of British subjects, and at the same time to establish themselves in self-governing independence in America. Accordingly, those of the promoters who wished to remain in England were induced to sell their holdings, and the remaining stock-holders with the whole government of the company, charter, records, capital and everything, left England with about 900 settlers and established their headquarters at Boston in Massachusetts.

Like Virginia, Massachusetts suffered great hardships in the early years, and like Virginia, it overcame them by virtue of a stern discipline. This discipline was enforced, however, not by old-soldier governors sent from England, but by a very able elected governor, and magistrates guided by the ministers and deacons of an uncompromising Church. Puritans in England for the most part had sought changes of government and ritual within the Church of England. In Massachusetts the Puritan movement became frankly separatist. This development affected politics, for the leading colonists quickly contrived to limit the colonial franchise to freeholders who were also accepted members of the separatist church. These were a comparatively small oligarchy; for many free-holders, though Calvinist in their religious beliefs, had no wish to leave the Church of England or to show disrespect to the Crown. In excluding these people from all political life except local town meetings, the rulers of the colony contravened English law and their own charter; but as Governor Winthrop pointed out, there was no democracy in Israel.

The government of Massachusetts was narrow, often unscrupulous, utterly lacking in humour, but extremely efficient. It quickly deported Thomas Morton, for instance, ostensibly for dancing round the maypole. Possibly Morton's maypole dancing was associated with witchcraft, which for a seventeenth-century Puritan was no subject for humour; but the Puritans were ruthless in punishing any kind of opposition or heterodoxy. This was a factor of some importance in the colonising of New England, for many people who quarrelled with the ruling oligarchy in Massachusetts over politics or religion were either expelled, or fled to escape worse punishments. These people founded new settlements such as Connecticut, New Haven, and Rhode Island, which grew and flourished modestly; though as time went on both Massachusetts and Connecticut began to develop an imperialism of their own and to swallow up the smaller settlements.

The expansion meant encroachment on Indian hunting grounds. The Massachusetts company, with its customary legalism, was careful to cover its acquisitions by purchase treaties. The Puritans were never enthusiastic missionaries; most of them apparently thought that the Indians were beyond hope, and like the Spaniards, they usually enslaved Indians captured in rebellion or frontier war. On the other hand, the company enforced those clauses in its charter forbidding the sale of firearms and liquor to the Indians. In this matter Christian conscience and common prudence pointed the same way. It is untrue to say that the Puritan settlers had no conscience where Indians were concerned; but their conscience for the most part worked in a purely negative way. They did not exploit the Indians, nor did they try to absorb them, but inexorably they pushed them aside.

In economic matters, the colonists concentrated doggedly upon immediately useful crops and made no attempt to fit into a theoretical scheme formulated in England. They could not grow sugar and they eschewed tobacco; but within twenty years they produced a surplus of food, which they sold to the Indians and later to the West Indian colonies. Of their main exportable products, timber was too bulky and awkward to be shipped across the Atlantic with much hope of profit. Transport costs were so high that New England timber could never compete with Baltic timber in the English market, despite a generous bounty. Most of the timber cut was used for building houses and ships in New England, but later a large quantity went to the West Indies in the form of barrel staves. Fur was a valuable article, in high demand in England; though as white settlement advanced inland the Indian trappers were driven before it, and New England fur became too scarce and expensive to compete with that which came down the Hudson and the St Lawrence. The New Englanders fished assiduously, and quarrelled and competed with the seasonal fleets which fished for the English and European markets. Some of the cod caught in New England ships went to Old England, some went direct to the Mediterranean countries; but much was consumed in New England by a population which increased year by year, for as the Laudian Church system tightened its grip upon England, so more and more Puritans emigrated to America. At the outbreak of the Civil War, Massachusetts had some 14,000 inhabitants and exercised most of the attributes of an independent state.

Mention must be made of a few fish, fur and timber colonies founded outside New England and without Puritan connections. The desire for secure bases for the fishery and the fur-trade inspired the planting of English settlements in Newfoundland, French settlements on the St Lawrence and the Bay of Fundy, and both French and Scottish settlements in Acadia, which is now Nova Scotia. The Newfoundland settlements were not at first particularly prosperous or particularly important, and they led to perpetual quarrelling over foreshore rights; but they survived, and developed as a permanent British colony. Sir William Alexander's Scottish settlement in Nova Scotia was less fortunate; it was only just founded in 1627, when war broke out between England and France. The war was a European dispute and had nothing to do with colonial matters, but of course it led to privateering warfare in the colonies and in 1629 the French settlers at Quebec surrendered to the English. At the time of the treaty of St Germain-en-Laye in 1632, therefore, the English were in control of all the settled parts of Canada, but in that treaty Charles I handed Quebec and Nova Scotia back to France,

and the development of Canada was left in the hands of French fur-
traders and Jesuit missionaries. Charles I and his advisers had no
inkling—why should they have?—of the future importance of the
St Lawrence estuary, nor of the lives and money which the English
were to spend in reasserting their interests in Canada.

8

RIVAL EMPIRES IN AMERICA

(i) *The French in Canada*

The French entered the colonial field at about the same time as the English and settled in the same sort of places on the Atlantic coast of North America and in the West Indian islands, places where the native population was relatively sparse and primitive. Like the English, the French could not hope to live on native tribute or to employ native labour on a large scale, and they found no precious metals. Like the English, they had to live by agriculture, by fishing, or by the fur trade in their northern possessions, and by growing tobacco or sugar in their West Indian islands. Like the English, they were keenly alive to the importance of sea power and the value of colonies as sources of naval stores and of tropical products. Like the English, they made great use of joint-stock companies of the commercial pattern for founding colonies.

The chronology of the development of French America corresponds closely to the English story. The moves of the two nations suggest either conscious mutual imitation, or the tactical counter-moves of the chess-board; and what a chess-board it was, both for size and for variety of pieces! The French, like the English, had engaged in exploring and privateering in American waters in the sixteenth century. French fishermen had regularly fished the Banks. Cartier and Roberval had explored the Bay of Fundy and the St Lawrence in the hope of finding a passage to the Pacific, and had tried to plant a colony, but without success. Other attempts were made in Central and South America; but both English and French first began to achieve permanent settlements in the early seventeenth century, after the end of the maritime war with Spain. Both

Henry IV and James I granted colonising monopolies in America. In 1605 a French Huguenot group founded Port Royal in Acadia. In 1608 the great Champlain, sailor, explorer, cartographer and scientist, founded the French settlement of Quebec. Acadia became a self-supporting colony of small farmers who in time enjoyed a modest prosperity. Quebec, on the other hand, was a trading station rather than a colony. Its inhabitants traded with the Indians for furs, which they shipped down the St Lawrence to France. Their capital, their trade goods, and most of their food came from France. They were backed by the Company of New France, which was incorporated by Richelieu and which sought to pay its shareholders out of the profits of the fur trade.

English and French settlers soon came to blows. In 1613 the Virginia Company organised an expedition which attacked Port Royal and actually destroyed an incipient French settlement on the coast of Maine. In 1627, as we have seen, the Nova Scotia Scots seized Port Royal, and in 1629 an English squadron intercepted the French food ships on their way up the St Lawrence and starved Quebec into surrender. The treaty of 1632 restored both places to France. Acadia was disputed ground through the seventeenth century, until 1714 when it went to England. Quebec remained in the hands of France until 1763, and is French in speech and tradition to this day.

The reign of Charles I and the ministry of Richelieu showed remarkable superficial resemblances in the colonial field, and saw the beginning of a bitter rivalry. There were also fundamental differences, however. Both rulers chartered a number of colonising companies; but in the English companies the initiative came from the promoters, who found their own capital and petitioned the King for charters. In France the initiative more often came from the government, which provided part of the capital and nominated some of the directors. Later, in Colbert's day, the government sometimes nominated all the directors and collected the capital by means of a kind of forced loan or compulsory investment. Obviously, where the Crown accepted these responsibilities, there was a great tendency for the government to supervise all the details of administration, and for the company to lean on the government for support. The Indian and other wars of the French colonies, for instance, were fought, not only by a colonial militia, but by regular troops sent from France.

The English charters on the whole maintained a difference between companies formed mainly for settlement and companies formed mainly for trade. Nearly all Richelieu's companies were general monopoly concerns which combined colonisation and trade. Inevitably they concentrated on the trade, which offered quick and certain profits, and neglected the colonisation. There was not much natural inducement for farmers, artisans and other solid citizens to leave a prosperous and victorious France and settle in a bleak and uninviting Canada; those who did settle found themselves at the mercy of a trading monopoly which demanded top prices for European goods. The manner in which settlement was organised also acted to some extent as a deterrent. The company granted *seigneuries*—block grants of land—mostly to directors of the company and their associates, many of whom were absentees. The intention was that the *seigneurs* should sub-let small-holdings in their grants on semi-feudal terms, retaining certain rights, as in France, including a limited right to the labour of their tenants. The company thus shuffled off its responsibility for settlement on to the *seigneurs*, and the settlers were under a constant temptation to leave their holdings and take to the woods as traders or trappers. The French were pre-eminent among Europeans in their capacity to live in the forest and to accept and share the life of the primitive Indians while they were there. Official French policy permitted and even encouraged mixed marriages. A small French and half-caste population ranged over tracts of country far bigger than it could occupy effectively; a fact which for a long time prevented Canada from becoming self-supporting, much less self-governing.

Charles I never put any serious obstacle in the way of Nonconformists, Catholic or Puritan, emigrating to America; but the French government, like the Spanish, refused to admit Protestants to its colonies. The consequences of this policy of religious purity were especially serious in France, because there, unlike Spain, the Huguenots were numerous and prosperous. Canada was denied a source of skilled and industrious colonists; and as their condition in France grew worse, the Huguenots tended to migrate to other countries, including England and the English colonies, so that there was a double loss both to Old and New France.

The ecclesiastical affairs of French America were largely in the hands of the Jesuits, probably the most efficient and determined missionary order in the whole history of Christendom. Jesuit methods involved living among the Indians and using their languages. Much territory on the shores of the Great Lakes was first explored by missionaries, many of whom suffered a gruesome martyrdom. The Jesuit ideal was to establish mission communities where Christian Indians could live a common life under priestly guidance, shielded from contact with *coureurs des bois* and other Europeans.

This segregation ran counter to the interests of the French settlers, who traded with the Indians for furs and supplied them with axes, knives, blankets, rum and firearms—arms sometimes used against the missionaries. Moreover, missionary work among the Hurons and Algonquins of the Lakes country embroiled the French with the hereditary enemies of those tribes, the powerful Iroquois confederacy of the Mohawk and upper Hudson valleys. The Iroquois, as fur-trading middle-men, tended in later years to ally themselves with the English, a factor of great importance in the subsequent wars, in which the wretched Hurons, with their thin veneer of Christianity, were almost wiped out.

When the great cardinal died, Canada had about three thousand white inhabitants, as against 20,000 or so in New England and perhaps 15,000 in Virginia. The work of empire-building was hardly begun. It fell to Colbert to reorganise New France and to give it that stamp of efficient military bureaucracy which it bore throughout the long wars with England. In this he achieved a considerable success; and the strength of his genius can be appreciated only if one remembers that, unlike his English counterparts, he served a king who cared nothing for trade or colonies and was interested only in military and religious glory in Europe.

(ii) *West Indian rivalries*

In the West Indies, as in North America, French and English settlement went on side by side. Sixteenth-century French enterprises such as the Huguenot settlement in Florida had been frustrated by the Spaniards; but in the sixteen-twenties the French, like the English, turned their attention to the islands of the Outer Antilles not occupied by Spain. In the early years relations between the two interloping races were comparatively friendly. In St Kitt's, indeed, a French and an English settlement grew up in close neighbourhood, being kept from fighting one another by common fear of the Caribs. The St Kitt's settlement was followed by other French colonies in Martinique and Guadeloupe, all of which were planted by a government-sponsored monopoly, the Company of the Isles of America. Richelieu himself put up a considerable proportion of the capital of this company, which, like the Company of New France, was both a colonising and a trading concern.

The story of these French islands is a close parallel to that of the English West Indies. Being suited to a plantation economy they proved much more attractive to French settlers than Canada did, and in the early years they outstripped Canada in trade with the home country just as Barbados outstripped New England. Like Barbados they produced first tobacco and then sugar. None of the French islands rivalled the prosperity of Barbados in the seventeenth century, but later they were to become more prosperous, partly because they contained a great area of virgin soil suited for extensive cultivation, partly because the French, unlike the English, allowed all the processes of sugar refining to be carried out in the colonies—obviously a sensible arrangement, though contrary to strict mercantile theory. The French planters employed as labour first white *engagés*—the equivalent of our indented servants—and subsequently Negro slaves. Later in the century the French, like the English, formed an Africa company to undertake the supply of slaves to the West Indies.

Like the Barbadians, the French West Indian planters believed that they were being exploited by the commercial fraternity of their own country; and they had the additional disadvantage of having to deal with a trading monopoly. Like the English, therefore, the French planters preferred to do business with the universal carriers, the Dutch, and in the middle years of the century they relied mainly on the Dutch, not only for slaves, but for a wide range of European manufactured goods. The Dutch traders profited by the fact that France, like Spain and in a lesser degree like England, had not enough shipping to handle the volume of trade which developed, and that the shipping they had was not sufficiently specialised.

The Dutch themselves founded colonies in the Caribbean; but as usual, settlement was for them a means to commercial ends rather than an end in itself. Their seizures of territory were intended to further the prosecution of maritime war against Spain and the establishment of a Dutch commercial monopoly. The Dutch West India Company was incorporated in 1621, upon the expiry of the uneasy twelve years' truce with Spain, and one of its avowed purposes was to wage maritime war and to make profits by plunder as well as by trade. The organisation of the company was an imitation of that of the East India Company. It was a subsidised monopoly; and in view of the growing importance of the slave trade its monopoly area was made to include the west coast of Africa. The monopoly was never effectively enforced; for the many private Dutch merchants trading in the West Indies would not withdraw from a profitable illicit commerce which they had built up by their own initiative. Probably the failure to appreciate the difference between conditions in the East and in the West Indies was the cause of many of the company's failures and of its ultimate bankruptcy in 1674.

In its early years, however, the Dutch West India Company at least succeeded in inflicting heavy damage on Spanish and Portuguese interests in America. Its first large-scale undertaking, the attempt to capture the sugar region of north-east Brazil from the Portuguese, began with an attempt on Bahía by a powerful fleet in 1624. In a decade of intermittent fighting, the Dutch spread their control of the Brazilian coast all the way from Recife to the Amazon. Their main object in establishing this control was to manipulate the trade of the region to their own commercial advantage. The company, however, was unwilling and unable to shoulder the expense and responsibility of maintaining adequate garrisons or of administering the territory. In the sixteen-forties, after the successful national revolt of Portugal against Spain, an independent rising took place in Brazil against the Dutch West India Company. By 1654 the last of the company's servants were expelled and in due course the Dutch abandoned their claims to all mainland territory except Surinam. Portugal at this time was a close ally, almost a client of England, and the trade of the Brazilian ports fell largely into the hands of English merchants. The most important and lasting result of this short-lived Dutch occupation of Brazil was the introduction of sugar cultivation into the Caribbean islands by Dutch traders.

Meanwhile, the fleets of the West India Company had been ravaging the Spanish settlements in the Caribbean on a scale hitherto unknown. Their most successful year was 1628, when their Admiral Piet Heyn, commanding a fleet of thirty-one ships, intercepted off Cuba the yearly convoy bound for Spain. The whole convoy, merchantmen, treasure ships and escort, fell into the hands of the Dutch. A Dutch admiral had at last won the prize which had been dreamed of by every sailor for seventy years. Spain's already failing credit in the international money-market received a blow from which it never recovered, and Spanish military and naval activity both in Europe and in the Caribbean was for a time almost paralysed.

Piet Heyn's great exploit was not to be repeated for another thirty years; it was followed, however, by a whole series of lesser, but still serious depredations by Dutch fleets. Nothing illustrates the strength and tenacity of the Spaniards' imperial administration more dramatically than their persistence in face of these disasters. Despite the constant burning and pillaging of their Caribbean ports, they surrendered no important stretch of territory, and they contrived somehow to send convoys across the Atlantic, though often at irregular intervals and at ever-increasing risk and expense More they could not do. For the rest of the seventeenth century they were powerless to prevent or to control the comings and goings of foreign ships in the Caribbean. Behind the fleets of the West India Company

ranged the swarm of Dutch private traders, and English and French
settlers. Illicit trade to the Spanish Indies grew year by year, and in
the hands of the ubiquitous Dutch came to outstrip the legitimate
traffic by five or six to one. At the same time English and French
colonists went where they would in the lesser Antilles and pursued
their planting enterprises without fear of Spanish interruption;
though Spain did not accept the principle of the freedom of the high
seas until after 1660, nor recognise as valid the titles of other powers
to their own West Indian settlements until the treaty of Madrid in
1670.

Apart from Brazil, the territorial acquisitions of the Dutch during
this period of bitter rivalry were small but valuable. The merchant
directors of the West India Company were well aware that the re-
ceipts from plunder could not cover the cost of large-scale naval
war over a long period. Fleets of warships could not be kept cruising
in the Caribbean indefinitely; the safety of Dutch merchant shipping required local bases, preferably island bases, since the expense
of defending a harbour on the Spanish Main itself would have been
prohibitive. The company found an ideal stronghold in the barren
island of Curaçao, lying off the coast of Venezuela and offering
easy access to every part of the Main. The islands of which Curaçao is the chief also offered an attraction in the form of natural salt
pans. Salt was needed in great quantities for the Dutch herring
fishery; formerly it had been imported from southern Portugal, so
that in time of war an alternative supply was doubly welcome. A
Dutch fleet seized Curaçao without opposition in 1634. The island
at once became the centre of Dutch power and commerce in the
West Indies and has remained so ever since.

The fighting ships which swarmed in the Caribbean were not all
warships. The long privateering war against Spain had sown
dragon's teeth throughout the West Indies. The buccaneers, the
rough cattle-hunters of the islands, took to piracy, throve and increased. Sailing from bases in Hispaniola, Jamaica and Tortuga, they
operated mainly against Spanish harbours and coastal shipping, but
as the century wore on they became an intolerable plague to the
honest enterprise of every nation. Often they sold their plunder in
New England with the connivance of the Boston and Salem merchants; for many, perhaps most of them, were Englishmen. The
attitude of the English government towards them varied with the
changes in Anglo-Spanish relations. In time of war, a government
could find ready employment for gangs of desperadoes in the Caribbean. In the treaty of Madrid in 1670, in return for Spain's recognition of the English West Indian possessions, the English govern-

ment undertook to disown and suppress the buccaneers; but they could find no better way of doing it than by appointing the buccaneer captain Henry Morgan as Lieutenant-Governor of Jamaica. Not until James II's day did the government attack the buccaneers in the only effective way; by the despatch of cruiser squadrons commissioned for the purpose. The French government dallied still longer; but by the end of the century the reign of terror was drawing to a close, and sea fighting in the Caribbean, though by no means at an end, was becoming the affair of regular naval forces.

(iii) *The Portuguese in Brazil*

At the time when Brazil was discovered, Portugal was a poor country with probably less than a million inhabitants. The Portuguese already had their hands full with their efforts to open trade with India. Their early settlements in Brazil were planted partly to serve as ports of call for the Indies fleets, partly to act as obstacles to Spanish attempts to settle within the Portuguese demarcation. These settlements remained small and poor throughout most of the sixteenth century; their only important exportable product was brazilwood, a somewhat inferior red dye.

The circumstance which, at the end of the sixteenth century, brought Brazil its first wave of prosperity was the tremendous growth in the European demand for sugar. Portuguese America was much better placed for sugar production than Spanish America; north-east Brazil offered vast areas of suitable land; the Portuguese had settlements in West Africa from which slaves could be obtained, and they possessed the shipping to carry the slaves. The settlers of northern Brazil included a considerable proportion of wealthy people from the north of Portugal, accustomed to the direction of large estates; and a prosperous large-scale plantation economy soon grew up round Bahía and Pernambuco. In the first half of the seventeenth century Brazil was the world's chief source of sugar, and reached its peak of prosperity when the rest of the Portuguese empire was declining under Spanish rule. It was the wealth derived from sugar which prompted the Dutch to make their attempt at conquest; and the successful war of the Portuguese colonists against the invaders may be regarded, perhaps, as marking the beginning of a feeling of national solidarity in the north of Brazil.

Portuguese colonial administration lacked the coherence and conscientious detail of that of Spain. In the early days of settlement the Portuguese Crown indifferently allowed an almost feudal state of

affairs to grow up in Brazil. A small number of noblemen—the captains-donatory—were granted huge tracts of territory to settle and
develop more or less as they pleased. After the union of the crowns
in 1580, however, Brazil became affected by Spanish ideas, and the
provincial captains were regarded, at least in theory, as royal officials
rather than as feudatories. A viceroy was appointed, first at Bahía,
later at Río de Janeiro. In 1604, a Portuguese Council of the Indies
was established, in imitation of the Spanish council, but sharing the
work of colonial administration with the Council of Finance. The
first Brazilian *audiencia*, that of Bahía, was set up in 1608. Even so,
the captains remained semi-independent in practice, legislation was
piece-meal, dealing with individual and local problems; there was
nothing comparable with the great colonial codes issued by the
Spanish Crown for the colonies of Spain. The protection of natives
—that perennial source of friction—was left largely in the hands of
the Jesuit order; it was only after the expulsion of the Jesuits in the
eighteenth century that the Portuguese government faced the problem of formulating a native policy. Thus while the administration of
seventeenth-century Brazil resembled that of Spanish America in
principle, in practice it was far less developed. Each captaincy lived
its own life, more or less independent of its neighbours, much as did
the English colonies of North America, owning only an ultimate
loyalty to the Crown.

In economic regulation, as might be expected, the Portuguese
government was more meticulous, and its legislation was more con-
sistently mercantilist than that of Spain. Like Spain, Portugal
claimed a monopoly of the trade of its colonies, and its merchant
shipping was more nearly adequate for the exercise of a monopoly.
The Portuguese government never tried, as the Spanish government
constantly did, to confine shipping to routes which were a defiance
both of geography and of common sense. Manufacture for export
was prohibited in Brazil, and so was the cultivation of vines and
olive trees; but on the other hands, some of the products of Brazil,
notably sugar, were encouraged by preferential customs in Portugal. In one respect Portuguese policy was less liberal than that of
Spain: printing and the production of books was forbidden in
Brazil.

In the second half of the seventeenth century Brazil began to lose
its lead in the production of sugar. This was due partly to soil exhaustion in the north-east, partly to the decline of the Portuguese
slave trade; for though the Dutch failed to conquer Brazil, they
succeeded, while Portugal was still under Spanish rule, in seizing
most of the Portuguese slave stations in West Africa. In Brazil itself,

sugar ceased to be the chief source of easy wealth, its place being taken at the end of the century by the gold of Minas Geraes. As a consequence, Río de Janeiro came to eclipse aristocratic Bahía. The lead in sugar production passed to the English and French West Indies, while the lion's share of the slave trade went first to the Dutch and later to the English.

(iv) *The Dutch on the high seas*

The Dutch West India Company possessed stations and colonies not only in South America and the West Indies, but on the Atlantic coast of North America also. New Netherland had first been planted early in the seventeenth century, and by the middle of the century it included a string of settlements up the Hudson as far as Albany, along the coast of Long Island Sound as far as the border of Connecticut, in Long Island and in New Jersey. Like most colonies run by trading concerns, New Netherland was very sparsely settled. Some Dutch settlers owned large estates, but they cultivated only small parts of them, and most of the settlements were mere trading stations. An English observer in 1663 put the population at 1,900, of whom about 600 were said to be Englishmen. New Netherland was not, therefore, a very formidable community in itself; but commercially it was of great importance. The Hudson was the highway for the fur trade of the interior and—though this was not realised at the time—the best ice-free gateway to Canada. New Amsterdam, the company's fort at the mouth of the Hudson, was the base and clearing-house for a great volume of Dutch shipping, which ran a carrying trade between the harbours of continental Europe and the Spanish, English and French colonies. The English Acts of Trade, of course, made it illegal for Dutch ships to enter English colonial harbours as it had always been illegal for them to enter Spanish American harbours, but the Dutch continued to make clandestine visits to both and were welcomed by the planters. It was easy, moreover, for New England ships to put into New Amsterdam, and lawful until 1660 for them to sell West Indian sugar, rum and tobacco to the Dutch. In return they bought large quantities of European goods—glass, bricks, paper, cloth and other manufactured articles—which had neither been bought in England nor paid English customs.

With their open port at New Amsterdam and their trading stations in the Caribbean, the Dutch were in a position to rob Spain, France and England of a great part of the commercial value of their colonial possessions; for they had also the shipping to carry the load. In commerce, especially in seaborne commerce, the Dutch in the seventeenth century were the masters and the teachers of Europe—not unnaturally, since trade was the whole life and livelihood of their state. Their East and West India companies were powerful state-subsidised corporations, and high office in one of the companies was socially as honourable as high office in the state itself. Many English writers paid envious tribute to Dutch superiority in trade. One, Joseph Hill, put into the mouth of a Dutch merchant this explanation:

'As to the capital, ours comes to be greater in regard that as the merchants grow rich in England they buy land and breed up their sons to be country gentlemen; whereas we . . . in Holland continue the stock and our children in the trade.'

Sir Josiah Child, the well-known English East India merchant, gave the following list of reasons for Dutch prosperity:

'Fidelity in their seal,' (that is, business honesty) 'encouragement of inventors, whom they reward, while they make the invention public, instead of granting a patent as here, thrift, small ships, low duties, poor-laws, banks, mercantile law, easy admission of burghers, inland navigation, low interest, fisheries, colonies, religious liberty, education.'

The Dutch ran their empire and their commerce with great efficiency and with careful attention to detail. Their capital was more fluid than the English, their business methods more up-to-date, their ships better designed. Although their own country produced none of the materials for ship-building, they commanded the mouth of the Rhine down which came the oak of Germany; their redemption treaty with Denmark in 1649, compounding for the payment of Sound dues, gave them easier access to the masts, planks, hemp and pitch of the Baltic countries; and they showed in the use of these imported materials a remarkable technical inventiveness. They built their ships to be handled by the smallest possible crews, reducing running rigging to the simplest essentials, using winches wherever possible to replace human strength. The Dutch developed fore-and-aft rig, an immense advance upon the lateen for beating to windward, long confined to boats and yachts, but introduced into big ships towards the end of the seventeenth century to supplement the square sails which supplied the main driving power. The Dutch, too, experimented with methods of protecting ships' hulls against marine borers, using first tallow and then lead sheathing—(copper was an eighteenth-century innovation).

It was the Dutch who first bravely and definitely abandoned the centuries-old compromise between the merchant packet and the man-of-war, relying upon convoy in case of need to protect un-armed ships. Their East Indiamen, it is true, retained with reason the heavy timbering and the galleried transom stern of ships built for fighting; but their characteristic mid-seventeenth-century general carrier, the *fluyt* or flyboat, was deliberately designed to carry goods, not guns. Its broad beam and flattened bottom, the round tuck of its stern, the restriction of cabin accommodation to a narrow after-superstructure, gave it maximum hold space combined with maximum economy of building material. In rig it was a small three-masted barque, with the usual lateen mizen. Its fore and main masts were characteristically stepped far apart, leaving room for capacious hatches. It was ugly but serviceable, cheap to build and economical to handle, a slow but safe sailer. Apart from the *fluyt*, the Dutch ex-celled in devising specialised types for particular trades—the 'buss' for the North Sea herring drifting, the sturdy, stump-masted whaler for the Greenland whale fishery, the timber-carrier with its great stern port and long hold. Dutch yards turned out thousands of medium-sized merchant ships of all kinds, not only for Dutch mer-chants, but for sale to English merchants too, despite the scandalised protests of Trinity House.

All these advantages had made the Dutch, by the middle of the seventeenth century, the general carriers of Europe. Amsterdam was a great city of warehouses from which all Europe was supplied with tropical and colonial goods. The Dutch had taken a leaf out of Sir John Hawkins's book. The planters of Virginia and Barbados pre-ferred to ship their tobacco and sugar in Dutch ships because the Dutchmen offered European goods at lower prices, longer credit and cheaper freight rates. It was said, too, that they understood the problems of stowage better and took greater care of their cargoes. The governor of Virginia said in so many words in the course of a speech in the colonial assembly: 'We can only fear the Londoners, who would fain bring us to the same poverty, wherein the Dutch found and relieved us.' That was in 1651, the year of the second Navigation Act.

The Navigation Act of 1651 was an act of economic war against the Dutch and in 1652 it led to real war; but Commonwealth policy towards the Dutch wavered. Cromwell could never rid his mind of the Spanish bogey. With the Dutch there was economic rivalry, but there was also religious and political sympathy. Even during the war, suggestions were being made for a kind of Anglo-Dutch 'Tordesillas' treaty. The Spaniards and Portuguese were to be dispossessed, and the whole colonial world was to be divided, the Dutch taking Brazil and the East, England the rest of the Americas. Other proposals were canvassed for a union between England and the United Provinces. None of these proposals came to anything, and eventually the anti-Dutch policy won the day. In 1654, at the end of the war, England arranged with Denmark its own composition for Sound dues and secured open access to the sources of Baltic timber; while the Dutch, though dropping their open protests against the Navigation Act, in fact continued their illicit trade with the English colonies, through the port of New Amsterdam. The English restoration government thus inherited a policy of economic war against the Dutch, and a conviction that, if any sort of economic unity was to be achieved in the English empire, the Dutch power in New Netherland must be destroyed.

THE OLD COLONIAL SYSTEM

(i) *The plantations in 1660*

The initiative in English colonisation, as in Spanish, had come from private individuals or groups, whether bands of adventurers or syndicates of merchants. In the second half of the sixteenth century the Spanish Crown had sought with considerable success to weld the Indies into a unified empire with a common administrative system. By the middle of the seventeenth century the time was ripe for the English government to attempt something of the kind in its own colonial possessions. Civil war and successive changes of government had weakened central authority and had affected different colonies in different ways. Barbados and the other islands had been staunchly royalist; they had surrendered to naval force at the end of the English civil war, but on the whole Parliament had left governors and assemblies to govern as best they might. Virginia was also royalist, though less unanimously so. In New England the colonial assemblies had naturally sympathised with the Puritan cause, but nevertheless had made it clear that parliamentary interference in their affairs would be no more welcome than royal interference. Massachusetts had set up a mint, annexed some of the territory of Maine and New Hampshire, and opened its harbours to the ships of all nations. At the Restoration the colonies had all acknowledged Charles II, but some had used very non-committal terms in doing so, and the Massachusetts assembly had passed a resolution claiming to be 'a body politick in fact and in name'.

The powers exercised by the Crown in different colonies varied considerably in fact and in law. Up to the Civil War, Virginia had been the only crown colony. During the war and interregnum several other grants lapsed or were suppressed. Barbados and the Leeward Islands became crown colonies, voting a permanent export duty to the home government in consideration of being quit of all proprietary claims. Jamaica had been captured by a formal naval operation, and after a few years of military rule, it naturally became a crown colony too. In all these colonies the Crown appointed the governors, executive councils, judges and other high officials. The councillors almost always, and sometimes the governor also, were resident planters, but more commonly the governors came from England. They were appointed by letters patent, held office during the King's pleasure, and like office-holders in England at the same time, regarded their offices as a form of property, sometimes as a form of investment. Unlike the Spanish *audiencias*, the colonial courts had no special powers; they administered common law, and appeal from their decisions lay to the Privy Council, not to any special court for colonial affairs.

The proprieties differed from the crown colonies in that in them the person of the proprietor was interposed between the Crown and the colonists. The proprietor was both landlord of his territory and head of its government. He appointed the governor and higher officials, and they took an oath of loyalty to him, not to the King. The proprietors were for the most part courtiers and there was never any question of proprieties setting up as independent states; in practice, the internal government of the proprieties was very like that of the crown colonies. By the middle of the century proprietary grants were widely felt to be anachronisms; only one of them—Maryland—survived the Civil War as a going concern, and the Privy Council constantly petitioned Charles II not to create any more. He did in fact grant several more: Carolina in 1663, to a syndicate; New York and New Jersey in 1664 to the Duke of York; and Pennsylvania in 1681 to the Quaker, William Penn. Pennsylvania was the first inland colony in English North America. The last English propriety to be granted in America was Georgia, founded in 1732 as a home for insolvent debtors.

The proprietary form of government never established itself in New England. The most serious attempt was that of Sir Ferdinando Gorges in Maine; and his heirs, shortly after the Restoration, sold their claim to the Massachusetts government. Massachusetts, Connecticut and (after 1663) Rhode Island were charter colonies; that is, they each possessed a royal charter similar in form to the charter of a joint-stock trading company, permitting the freeholders of the colony to elect their officers in the same way that the shareholders of a company did. There were no officials appointed by the Crown, and no representatives in England upon whom the Crown could bring pressure. Charter colony government was the nearest approach to responsible government in any of the colonial empires of the time.

In spite of these wide differences in the relation of colonies to the Crown, there existed by 1660 a general pattern of internal colonial government, nowhere prescribed in law but everywhere recognised in practice. Every colony had a governor and an executive council; nearly every colony had an elected legislative assembly—the chief exception was New York, which had no assembly until 1689. The franchise was limited in all the colonies to freeholders; indented servants and landless people generally had no vote, except in town government, which was democratic in the classical sense of the word. Slavery, though its practical importance varied greatly, was recognised by law in all the colonies and caused liberty-loving Englishmen no serious searchings of conscience.

The English empire was the only European colonial empire at that time in which representative institutions played any significant part, as indeed was natural, since England, unlike Spain and France, embarked upon the settlement of colonies in a period when the idea of representative government was gaining strength in the mother country. Colonial assemblies voted taxes and made local laws; but after the Restoration, the crown lawyers began to argue that colonial Acts must be approved not only by the governor, but also by the Privy Council.

The English parliament legislated for the empire as a whole, particularly in matters of trade; it did not concern itself with the internal affairs of individual colonies, and the validity of its enactments was sometimes disputed, especially in New England. Colonial assemblies, however, could be required by the Crown or by Parliament to pass Acts. In some crown colonies the assemblies were even induced to pass perpetual Revenue Acts, such as the $4\frac{1}{2}$ per cent on tobacco in Virginia, which money was used to pay the salaries of governors and other officials. The constitutional position of the colonial assemblies in general was much less secure than that of the English parliament; but like Parliament they tended to encroach on the royal prerogative, and one of the characteristics of a good governor was his ability to manage and placate an intractable assembly.

The jealousies and the differences in loyalty between colony and colony; the independent language used by some colonial assemblies; the insolent disregard of royal orders in Massachusetts and elsewhere; the difficulty of enforcing trade regulation; all these circumstances seemed to demand the assertion of a unifying royal authority.

Economic and social considerations pointed the same way. The seventeenth century had brought greater prosperity and economic stability to England; developing industries created a demand for labour; emigration was no longer encouraged as a means of drawing off surplus population. Evelyn expressed the new attitude in a pamphlet of 1674 by referring to 'the ruinous numbers of our men daily flocking to the American plantations, whence so few return . . . which in time will drain us of people, as now Spain is, and will endanger our ruin as the Indies do Spain'. To outweigh the disadvantages of emigration, a colony must produce goods in demand in England and not capable of being produced there. The ideal colony was one where a small number of English planters supervised a large non-English labour force, whether slave or free, in producing tropical commodities; hence the various schemes put forward for prohibiting further emigration to New England, or shifting people from New England to the West Indies. Clearly, if colonisation and emigration were to be properly regulated in accordance with these theories, there would have to be a much stronger and more unified control at the centre.

(ii) *The Acts of Trade*

English government in the seventeenth century sought deliberately to make the colonies the economic counterpart of England in a unified empire; the whole being rendered, by the specialisation of its various parts, a stronger competitor in time of peace and a more powerful adversary in time of war. The chief dangers to the empire, in the opinion of Restoration statesmen, lay in the existence of economic war and the possibility of real war with the Dutch; in the widespread trading with foreigners in the colonies; and in the alleged indifference of the colonists to English interests. The colonial legislation of the later Stuarts was devised specifically to guard against these dangers, but it embodied also a general constructive policy. The long series of acts which made up the 'old colonial system' reflected the best economic theory of the time and were based on definite and consistent principles.

The colonies were to be given a monopoly of the home market for their characteristic products. This principle was early applied to Virginia tobacco, and extended in due course to most of the staple products of the colonies.

The colonies, having been founded for the benefit of the mother country, were to produce goods which England could not produce, in particular certain kinds of raw materials. Activities such as iron-working and felt-making in New England and sugar refining in the West Indies were to be discouraged.

All exports of the most valuable colonial products were to be sent to England. It seemed reasonable that if colonial producers were to be given a guaranteed market in England, then England could insist on a corresponding monopoly.

England was to control the carrying trade. The successes of the Dutch apparently defied free competition; strangers must therefore be excluded from the colonial market by law and by force, and exports and imports of the colonies must be confined to English or colonial ships.

The colonies were to be outside the fiscal boundaries of England. The system was one of empire preference, not one of empire free trade, for the Crown could not afford to forgo its dues. Colonial products always paid customs, though in most cases the duties were lower than those levied on comparable foreign goods, and in the case of re-export to the continent of Europe, part of the duty might be repaid in the form of a 'drawback'.

The navy and the merchant marine were to be enlarged. It was useless to proclaim a monopoly of colonial trade unless the empire had the ships to carry that trade; and the colonies could not be expected to submit to a monopoly unless the navy were strong enough to enforce the system, to protect colonial territory from attack, and to defend shipping from pirates and privateers.

Among the many Acts and orders embodying these principles three statutes stood out as the legal foundations of the whole system. These were the Navigation Act of 1660, the Staple Act of 1663 and the Plantations Duties Act of 1673. The colonial sections of the Navigation Act provided that no goods should be imported into or exported from any English colony except in English ships; that is, in ships built, owned and at least three-quarters manned in England or an English plantation. This provision was little more than a repetition of the earlier and largely ineffective Act of 1651. The 1660 Act, however, contained another clause which was new and original; this was the famous enumeration clause, providing that tobacco, sugar, cotton, indigo, ginger and dye-woods produced in the colonies should be shipped only to England or to another English colony. With the exception of tobacco, these were all West Indian products which could not be produced in England. The products of New England were not enumerated, either because they competed with English products, or because they could not be imported into England at a profit. The enumeration clause was enforced by a system of bonds. An English or colonial captain in the colonial trade was required to deposit a personal bond at his port of departure, as security that he would not carry enumerated goods to an illegal destination. The bond could be recovered later, on production of a certificate from the port of arrival, showing that the voyage had, in fact, complied with the law.

The Navigation Act left colonial ships perfectly free to engage in inter-colonial trade, and the bond system worked in such a way as to give them a virtual monopoly of this trade—in sharp contrast to the arrangements in the Spanish empire, where inter-colonial trade was controlled and hampered to the point of prohibition.

The Staple Act of 1663 dealt with colonial imports, and laid down that all goods, English or foreign, intended for the colonies, must be shipped from an English port. A few commodities, much in demand in America, were excepted from this rule, the most important being salt for the Newfoundland and New England fisheries, and the wines of Madeira and the Azores—colonies of Portugal, itself at that time a close ally and almost a commercial dependency of England. The Staple Act was intended to benefit the Crown by increasing the yield of the customs, the English exporters by protecting their colonial market, and above all the navy, by confining colonial trade to shipping lanes radiating from England, which could more easily be patrolled and protected.

The Plantations Duties Act laid a substantial export duty on all enumerated commodities shipped from one colony to another. Before the Act, colonial goods, ostensibly consigned to other colonies, could be carried to foreign ports and sold more cheaply than goods which had paid English customs. By imposing a duty at the port of departure, it was hoped to make such breaches of the Navigation Act unprofitable. The principles embodied in these statutes were confirmed and strengthened by the 1696 Navigation Act, which established admiralty courts in the colonies for the better enforcement of the law. They governed the economic structure of the old empire for over a century.

The 1660 Navigation Act was followed by so rapid a development of the English merchant marine that admiring economists of the time called the Act the 'Sea Magna Carta'. To what extent the Acts of Trade assisted this development is still an open question. That they were not a dead letter, is proved by the sustained protests of the Dutch through diplomatic channels, and of the West Indian planters through their agencies in London. The very efficient merchant marine of the new England colonies also grew and flourished under the protection of the Acts, and of the constant naval supervision which the Acts required. Naval protection was real and necessary. The North Atlantic was infested with pirates, not only the freebooting outlaws of the Caribbean, and not only Dutch or French privateers in time of war, but powerful fleets maintained by the North African sultans for the purpose of preying upon European shipping. In one year, 1679, Algerine pirates operating off the Scilly Isles took thirteen Virginia ships. The sugar ships from Barbados often had to sail north-about on their way to London; and many an English or colonial sailor ended his days pulling an oar in an Algerine galley. England maintained constant naval patrols along the main shipping routes, and even for a time a fleet base at Tangier. Sometimes by force, sometimes by treaty, it extracted from the sultans short-lived promises of immunity for English and colonial ships. A frigate squadron was based on Jamaica for operations against the West Indian buccaneers; and of course convoy escorts were provided during the wars with the Netherlands and with France.

Sea power was the key to English imperial policy. The need of naval protection induced the colonists to accept, at least in principle, the restrictions imposed by the Acts of Trade, and sea power enabled the English government to a considerable extent to enforce the Acts. There were two chief obstacles to complete enforcement: one, the strategic position of the Dutch on the Hudson; the other, the lack of local co-operation. In New England especially, the elected governors made little attempt to enforce the law where it conflicted with local interests. They obstructed the captains of H.M. ships in the performance of their duty, while to the Privy Council they returned smooth but evasive answers. They sought advantage without obligations, as the Privy Council minutes constantly complained. 'New England is become the great mart and staple by which means the navigation of the Kingdom is prejudiced, the King's revenue inexpressibly impaired, the price of home and foreign commodities lessened, trade decreased, and the King's subjects much impoverished.'

(iii) *New York and New England*

Colonial quarrels in the seventeenth century were to a considerable extent outside the orbit of normal diplomacy in Europe, and according to the notions of the time, the constant Dutch infringements of the Acts of Trade justified retaliation, without the formality of war. Charles II made no declaration of war when, in 1664, he granted all the territory between Connecticut and Maryland as a propriety to James, Duke of York—a capable sea commander and an able colonial administrator. James fitted out a fleet under the command of a professional soldier named Nicolls, who was instructed to annex New Netherland and also to hold an inquiry into the government of New England; the two questions obviously being, from a commercial point of view, closely connected. The annexation was carried out without resistance, and the Dutch settlers were given generous terms. Neither they nor the Netherlands government made much protest. New Amsterdam became New York; New York, New Jersey and Delaware became proprietary colonies; the English gained a back door into French Canada, though neither they nor the French seemed to grasp the full implications at the time; and the biggest leak in the English colonial trade system was stopped.

The other leak—New England smuggling—called for other methods. It was obvious that the Acts of Trade could be thoroughly enforced in the colonies only by English officials appointed and paid by the Crown. This meant an end of constitutional semi-independence. Accordingly, we find the Lords of Trade discussing, not merely economic regulation, but in general 'the necessity of bringing those people under a more palpable declaration of their obedience to His Majesty'. The Restoration governments sought at first to strengthen colonial administration in two ways: by converting the proprieties into crown colonies and by inserting royal officials into the charter colonies. The revocation of a proprietary patent was largely a matter of finding a legal loophole. The colonists had no great love for their proprietors, who were usually absentees, or for the rents which the proprietors charged; they were willing enough to come under crown administration. New Hampshire and Bermuda became crown colonies in Charles II's reign; New York, New Jersey and Delaware followed in 1685 by the fact of their proprietor becoming king. From 1689 the Crown insisted on controlling the appointment of governors, so weakening the power of the remaining proprietors. The growth of population in the colonies was making proprietary government an obvious anachronism, and the few proprieties which survived into the eighteenth century became bywords for corruption and incompetence.

In the charter colonies the situation was very different. The colonists, or at least the ruling oligarchies among them, were jealously attached to their charters, and might take up arms to defend them. Nicolls's commission was frustrated at every point. In 1677 the Massachusetts assembly wrote openly to the Privy Council:

'We humbly conceive, according to the usual sayings of the learned

in the Law, that the laws of England are bounded within the four seas
and do not reach America . . . not being represented in Parliament we
have not looked at ourselves to be impeded in our trade by them.'

In the same year they imposed upon their officials an oath of fidelity
to the colony which preceded the oath of allegiance to the King.

No imperial government, however preoccupied at home, could
ignore so open a challenge. In 1678, the first crown official was
appointed—Edward Randolph, as collector of customs for New
England. Randolph struggled for four years to enforce the Acts of
Trade in the teeth of organised obstruction. In 1683 he returned
to England in fury and at last stirred up the departments concerned
to start *quo warranto* proceedings against the Massachusetts charter.
The substance of the charges was that the colony had aspired to
become an independent body politic. In 1648 the charter was
annulled; after fifty-five years of self-government Massachusetts
came for the first time under crown administration. Connecticut and
Rhode Island followed shortly afterwards.

There was no resistance; when it came to the point, the New
Englanders preferred submission with protection to a precarious independence. The abrogation of the charters led logically to the union
of the northern colonies, for purposes of administration and defence,
in a single dominion. James II sent out a loyal and capable soldier,
Sir Edmund Andros, as governor-general of New England and New
York. Andros was to suspend the colonial assemblies and to govern
through a nominated council. In many respects his instructions resembled those issued to the Spanish colonial viceroys, especially
where they concerned the courts and the arrangements for judicial
appeals to England. However unacceptable constitutionally, the
experiment was a promising one from the point of view of administration. But in 1688, James lost his crown; there was a corresponding revolution in New England; Andros was arrested and
shipped home, the colonial assemblies resumed their sittings, and
the old separate jurisdictions and jealousies reappeared. A series
of compromises followed the accession of William III. Connecticut and Rhode Island, which had never given much trouble, recovered their charters in 1690. Massachusetts, the most recalcitrant
colony, also recovered its charter, but in a modified form; the governor was to be appointed by the Crown and the church membership
test for the franchise was to be abolished.

In the years immediately after the Revolution the government of
the English colonies in America assumed the form which it was to
retain until independence. The Crown had failed to achieve James

II's administrative ideal, of great centralised viceroyalties governed from Whitehall. The efforts of the later Stuarts had, however, brought about a certain measure of centralised control. The Crown now appointed governors and some other officials in nearly all the colonies. A customs organisation had been introduced, backed by vice-admiralty courts to enforce the Acts of Trade; and the feudal powers of the few remaining proprietors had been whittled away. In 1696, William III set up a permanent Board of Trade and Plantations to replace the more or less standing committees of the Privy Council which had hitherto looked after colonial affairs; though executive power remained, as before, with the Privy Council itself. On the popular side, the old representative system had also attained considerable uniformity. Every colony now had its elected assembly. The assemblies were important, of course, as nurseries of future independence; but meanwhile they often served to impede administration and to perpetuate inter-colonial quarrels. The governors were not responsible to the assemblies and inevitably the assemblies often behaved irresponsibly.

Apart from the lack of responsible government and the prevalence of inter-colonial rivalry, the old imperial system had one cardinal weakness: it never made proper arrangements for the payment of its officials. In some of the old crown colonies—Virginia and Barbados—the assemblies had been induced at an early date to grant to the Crown a permanent revenue by indirect taxation; but most of the assemblies obstinately refused to do this. They voted taxes year by year, and out of those taxes the governors and other officials had to be paid. Colonial governors naturally varied in character and ability. Some were great noblemen, some serving soldiers, some leading planters in the colonies, and some mere time-servers and greedy place-men. Nearly all were frustrated in their efforts at sound administration by the lack of an assured income. Their salaries were at the mercy of capricious assemblies, to which they were not responsible and which they could control only with great difficulty. It is not surprising that most of them took bribes in one form or another; and that English colonial government in the eighteenth century, though not oppressive, was often incompetent and corrupt.

One chief factor held the empire together—apart, of course, from old associations. That was the fear of invasion or encirclement. The Dutch possessions in North America had been swallowed up, but the Spaniard still ruled the largest and richest of the New World empires; the French colonies in the later seventeenth century were growing in power and population and appeared as dangerous adversaries in the north and west; the Indians were still a perpetual menace on the frontiers; and at the end of the century it seemed possible that all three might combine against the English on the Atlantic seaboard.

(iv) *Louisiana and Hudson's Bay*

The policy of Colbert in New France was a mercantilism more rigid and consistent than that of the English Restoration governments, and in some ways it achieved a more apparent, if temporary, success. His general aims may be grouped under three heads: first, a great increase in emigration to the colonies, making them self-supporting in food production and populous enough to resist attack, to offer a market for French goods and to produce colonial commodities wanted in Europe; second, a great increase in the merchant marine, to enable it to carry all the trade of the French empire and to conserve and extend French resources of timber, hemp, and other naval stores; third, the occupation of a string of strategic points with adequate military force, to enable France to block English expansion inland and to control the main waterways of North America. This last plan developed and expanded as the waterways were explored.

French colonisation at this stage was far more planned and regimented, far less spontaneous, than English or even Spanish expansion—for the Spaniards, too, were expanding in New Mexico and up the Pacific coast. Colbert's programme was on paper the widest and most ambitious of all the European colonising schemes in America. To put it into effect he first made a number of administrative changes. He abolished Richelieu's companies and at first entrusted American trade and settlement to a single corporation, the Company of the West. This mammoth company was to control West Africa, too. It was to operate, not as an independent trading concern, but as a crown agent. Subsequently, in 1678, the powers of the company fell in to the Crown, governing directly, so that by that date Colbert had done in the French empire what James II failed to do in the English. In the colonies, the military governors were to be assisted and at the same time watched by civil governors—*intendants*—who were to handle all financial and economic business. Governors and *intendants* together were to be advised by nominated councils which also served as courts of appeal, though they had none of the independent powers of the Spanish *audiencias*. The system was simpler and cheaper than the elaborate bureaucracy of Spanish America, and quicker and more efficient than the creaking English representative system.

Colbert retained the system of feudal *seigneuries* established in Richelieu's day, but made them conditional upon effective occupation. Everything possible was done to attract eligible settlers. Demobilised soldiers were pensioned with land for farms in Canada and were settled in considerable numbers along the Richelieu river and at other strategic points. Tools, seed and stock were provided at government expense. A paternal government was even prepared to provide settlers with wives; for French girls who were willing to marry settlers and who possessed adequate certificates of moral character were given passage to Canada, also at the expense of the government. These provisions were not without effect; the population of French Canada trebled during the Colbert régime. Even so, at his death in 1683, the total number was only about 10,000. The subsequent great increase was due more to the fecundity of the settlers than to a steady increase in emigration. The military efficiency of the population was very high in proportion to its political and economic primitiveness. The settlers were at once adventurous and disciplined, and their liability to military service was a reality, in sharp contrast with the English colonial militias, which were divided among a dozen separate governments, seldom mustered, and accustomed to cavil at the orders, or rather the entreaties, of the King's representatives.

As explorers by land, the French in America at this time far outshone their English contemporaries. By 1673 the Jesuits had completed the exploration of the Great Lakes and were striking southwards to the headwaters of the Mississippi and its affluents. In 1682 La Salle made his great journey by water down the whole length of the Mississippi to the Gulf of Mexico and opened up a whole vista of strategic and economic possibilities. La Salle lost his life in 1687, while still a young man, in a premature attempt to plant the colony of Louisiana at the mouth of the Mississippi. His adventurous imagination presented to his countrymen the project of connecting Louisiana with Canada by a chain of French settlements. The whole distance could be covered by several alternative water routes, with comparatively short portages. Communications could be safeguarded by forts covering the principal portages and the narrowest stretches of water. Nothing came of La Salle's dream in the seventeenth century, for Colbert's death in 1683 was followed by a period of stagnation and neglect in the colonial policy of France; but in the eighteenth century the project was pursued with great vigour, and might have set rigid limits to the slow westward expansion of English settlement, had the French in America been more numerous.

The courage and initiative of explorers are not enough, in themselves, to found an enduring empire. Even Colbert failed to make the solid work of settlement attractive to adventurous Frenchmen, for the restrictive feudal structure of Canadian settled society constantly drove the leading spirits out to the wilder frontiers. At the same time, the lucrative monopolies of the trading companies attracted interlopers, who were often the companies' dismissed or disgruntled servants. Two such malcontents were largely responsible for the most severe blow which befell the French monopoly in Canada in the seventeenth century—the foundation of the English Hudson's Bay Company. An overland route to the shores of Hudson's Bay was first discovered by two French fur traders, Radisson and Groseilliers. These men tried, but failed, to persuade the authorities in Quebec and in France to develop a trade in furs from Hudson's Bay; but they found a backer in England, in the person of Prince Rupert. The result was the incorporation, in 1670, of the Hudson's Bay Company, trading directly to the Bay by sea. This enterprise was the first serious attack on French leadership in the fur trade; and is the only Stuart incorporation which survives as a working concern today.

Twelve years of financial good fortune followed the company's foundation, and in those years forts were established to exploit the trade of the whole southern and south-western shore of the bay. Serious French counter-attacks began in 1682. In the general war following the English revolution of 1688 the French achieved widespread success. Frontenac, able and vigorous governor of Canada, recaptured Nova Scotia, overrun by the New Englanders in 1691, frightened the Iroquois tribes into temporary peace, and kept the frontiers of New England and New York in constant fear of combined French and Indian raids. Much of the bitterness of colonial warfare arose from this habit of employing Indian auxiliaries, with their naturally barbarous methods of fighting, and of torturing prisoners. At the same time a brilliant sea commander, D'Iberville, ravaged the English settlements in Newfoundland and all but destroyed the company's hold in Hudson's Bay. The favourable colonial terms secured by France in the treaty of Ryswick were due largely to the work of these men.

By the end of the seventeenth century the general lines of the final struggle for power and trade in America were already apparent. The Dutch were beginning to drop out, weakened by unequal war in Europe. The power of Portugal was localised in Brazil and unlikely to expand elsewhere. To some observers, at least, the Spanish empire seemed on the verge of collapse. In fact, despite commercial weakness and a top-heavy bureaucracy, it was to outlast the others as an imperial unity; but its part in the eighteenth-century struggle was to be largely passive. Of the major fighting competitors, each had its weaknesses. The English empire obviously suffered from lack of unity and discipline; but the French empire had the more serious defect of lack of people.

I O

TRADE AND DOMINION IN THE EAST

(i) *Exploration and expansion in the Far East*

Like most trading corporations, the Dutch East India Company acquired territorial possessions slowly and with reluctance. Theorists and politicians in Amsterdam attributed the decline of Portuguese power in the East to the dissipation of energy and capital in territorial conquest, and warned the Dutch company against a similar mistake. The official policy of the directors was to stick to trade and to avoid entanglement in Indonesian politics. This policy made it difficult to secure the Dutch factories against attack from the landward side. Coen, by stalling off the English challenge and by repelling the attacks of the Sultans of Bantam and Mataram in 1618–19, had rendered Batavia temporarily safe; but throughout most of the seventeenth century the Dutch could not venture far from the town without danger from Bantamese dacoits and kidnappers. There was little attempt at cultivation. Bounties continued to be claimed for the killing of tigers and rhinoceroses in the near neighbourhood, and Batavia depended for its food supply upon imports from Mataram.

Despite the directors' caution, some of the ablest of the company's officers in the East favoured a more acquisitive policy almost from the start. Coen himself declared the section of Java from the frontier of Bantam to that of Cheribon, and from the Java Sea to the Indian Ocean, to be Company's territory. He could not enforce his claim, and neither the directors nor the Indonesian princes took it seriously; but some of his more energetic successors—van Diemen and Speelman particularly—made far wider claims, and eventually their policy prevailed. Circumstances compelled the company to secure commercial mastery by means of territorial dominion.

The general plan inherited from Coen by his successors was to make Batavia a central mart for inter-Asiatic trade, and the general warehouse of Eastern goods for export to Europe. Since Dutch commercial interests extended throughout the East from Magasaki to the Persian Gulf, the plan of forcing trade through Batavia involved much unnecessary sea transport by long indirect routes; but as usual at that time, considerations of convenience were expected to give way to considerations of monopoly. A centralised monopoly was the easiest to protect. As a monopolist, the company sought to close the eastern seas, as far as possible, to all European ships except its own; and to confine native Asiatic shipping to an auxiliary rôle, of supplying local products without competing in the carrying trade on the main routes. Such a system could be enforced only by armed fleets, and maintained only through a vast network of fortified posts. The establishment of posts and bases called for treaties with the local rulers; commercial treaties led to alliances, and alliances to protectorates. Eventually the Dutch found themselves following in the footsteps of the Portuguese, but acquiring far more actual territory than the Portuguese had ever possessed.

One of the most obvious and immediate objects of the company's policy was to secure control of the western approaches to the archipelago. Batavia itself commanded the Sunda Strait. The other frequented gateway, the Malacca Strait, was commanded by the old Malayan port of Malacca, the last stronghold of the Portuguese in the East Indies. Malacca had already lost much of its trade through the competition of Batavia; Governor-general van Diemen took it in 1641, so making the western part of the Java Sea a well-guarded Dutch preserve. In the previous year, 1640, the Dutch had fastened their grip upon Ceylon, allying themselves with the King of Kandy against the Portuguese. The Sinhalese monarch, like many of the Indonesian princes, incurred a heavy war debt to the company, which he paid in instalments of elephants and cinnamon. The Dutch seized the coastal settlements, Colombo, Galle, Batticaloa, Trincomalee, and by 1658 the last Portuguese were expelled. Ceylon had long been an important half-way house of Indian Ocean trade. Dutch control of its most important harbours placed the company in a strong position to monopolise the trade routes across the Bay of Bengal and to discourage—though not, indeed, to prevent—other European trade with the Coromandel coast.

All these developments served to assure the Dutch monopoly of the most valuable part of the Eastern trade—the trade in spices with the Moluccas; for though the Spaniards hung on at Tidore until 1663, they were clearly fighting a losing battle. Of the principal spice-producing islands, the Banda group had been conquered by Coen in 1621; the inhabitants had been killed or reduced to slavery and their land distributed among the company's servants or nominees, who undertook to sell all their produce to the company at the company's prices. Amboina was similarly absorbed in 1647, after a long series of *hongi* raids by armed fleets of native mercenaries, employed by the Dutch to destroy all clove production in excess of the company's requirements. In 1650 a rising against the Dutch residents at Ternate led to reprisals there, and in 1657 the Sultan of Ternate was compelled to an agreement whereby, in return for a Dutch pension, he undertook to prohibit the cultivation of spices in all the islands subject to him; leaving spice-growing entirely to islands in the possession of the company. This agreement proved easier to sign than to enforce, for as Ternate came more and more under Dutch control, the local authority and prestige of its ruler declined, while the neighbouring principality of Macassar rose in importance as a commercial and political rival. Native traders from Macassar plied boldly among the islands and proved extremely difficult to intercept. English, Danish and Portuguese interlopers provided the ruler of Macassar with arms and ammunition for the inevitable war with the company. Nevertheless, in the series of conflicts which ensued Macassar was taken by a Dutch fleet and a large force of Buginese mercenaries under Cornelius Speelman. In 1669 the Dutch occupied the town and harbour. The ruler agreed to sell all the exportable produce of his dominions to the company, and granted the Dutch a monopoly of the import of manufactures and all Chinese goods. All these aggressions, though they strengthened the company's grip upon the trade of the archipelago, also had the effect of driving native ship-owners into a career of piracy. To protect their trade the Dutch had to establish more and more fortified posts, from Ternate in the Moluccas to Palembang in Sumatra.

In the smaller islands, except in the Banda group and at Amboina, the Dutch in the seventeenth century occupied only the port towns, or in some cases only the actual sites of forts and warehouses. But in Java political circumstances compelled them to expand territorially. The safety of Batavia at first depended largely upon the ability of the Dutch to exploit the rivalry between Mataram and Bantam, the two principal Muslim sultanates of Java. As a maritime state, Bantam had backed the losing cause of the English in 1618, in the hope of recovering the Batavia territory; and for both political and commercial reasons the Bantamese remained bitterly opposed to the Dutch. Mataram, by far the larger and more powerful of the two sultanates, was primarily a land power in the centre of

Java. It claimed Batavia and its hinterland by virtue of a general overlordship; but its rulers were torn between their dislike of the company's presence in Java, their contempt for the Dutch as mere merchants, and their desire to profit from the Dutch as customers for Mataram rice. For twenty years or so the *Susuhunan*—'he-to-whom-everything-is-subject'—of Mataram kept Batavia in constant anxiety. The conquest of Malacca, however, greatly weakened the position of the Javanese princes; and in 1646 a new *Susuhunan*, in return for recognition of his suzerainty, agreed to the exclusion of Javanese traders from the Spice Islands. Thirty years of comparative peace followed. In 1675 the Dutch, concerned about their food supply, intervened in a succession dispute in Mataram, and secured from the victor an agreement closing the Mataram ports to all other foreigners, granting a monopoly of the opium trade, and ceding a considerable tract of inland rice-producing territory to the company. Another succession war, in 1705, in much the same way brought the company yet more territory in Priangan and East Madura, and suzerainty over Cheribon. These regions had formerly been claimed by Bantam; but the company had picked a quarrel with Bantam in 1680, and after inflicting a crushing naval defeat upon the Sultan, had insisted on his abandoning his territorial claims, granting a pepper monopoly to the Dutch and closing his ports to other foreigners. By the end of the century, the company not only controlled all the ports of Java, but possessed a great tract of inland territory from coast to coast; and no native prince dared challenge its position.

In the second half of the seventeenth century the company definitely established its naval, commercial and political supremacy in the islands, and all the major Indonesian principalities collapsed. Powerful, warlike and civilised though they were, they proved no match for the Dutch company with its stable organisation, its freedom from succession troubles and its inexorable demand for profit. Constantly troubled by harem intrigues and succession wars, the Indonesian princes called all too readily upon the Dutch to intervene in their quarrels. Every service performed in this way by the Dutch was rewarded with commercial concessions, which strengthened the company's command of the surrounding sea. Although the directors disliked political and territorial entanglements, the company's officers, once they became involved in a quarrel, never failed to see it through until their expenses had been repaid with handsome interest. By the end of the century, although the territory administered by the Dutch was still comparatively small, a much greater area was covered by states which had become virtually Dutch protectorates. Their trade was already firmly subordinated to Dutch needs. The way was prepared for widespread annexation and the development of a great territorial empire in the eighteenth century.

Although the intentions of the Dutch were chiefly commercial, their voyages obviously added greatly to European geographical knowledge, The sixteenth-century world-maps of Mercator and Ortelius, still influenced by Ptolemy, had marked a vast continuous land mass, *Terra Australis Incognita,* separated only by straits from South Africa and South America. Drake's great voyage, however, proved Tierra del Fuego to be an island, and not a peninsula. In the seventeenth century, east-bound Indiamen found thousands of miles of open water between the thirties and forties of south latitude in the Indian Ocean. Nothing was then known of the real Antarctic continent. Ptolemy's *Terra Australis* therefore retreated to the southern extremity of some maps and disappeared entirely from others. Meanwhile, however, the real Australia had been discovered as an incidental result of Dutch expansion in the East. Australia was probably unknown to Europeans until a series of captains, mostly Dutch, chanced upon its coasts in the early years of the seventeenth century. Willem Janszoon touched the coasts of New Guinea and north-eastern Australia in 1606, but thought them part of the same land mass. The first navigator to use the Torres Strait between Australia and New Guinea—without, however, appreciating the nature of the discovery—was the Spaniard who gave his name to the Strait, also in 1606. Two other Dutchmen, Hartogszoon and Houtman, in 1616 and 1619, discovered and explored part of the coast of south-western Australia. In 1642, under the governorship-general of van Diemen, Abel Tasman sailed from Batavia to Mauritius, thence round Australia, along the north coast of New Guinea and back to Batavia by way of the Macassar Strait. Tasman discovered Tasmania and New Zealand. He never actually sighted the coasts of Australia on this voyage; but his discoveries set definite limits to the area in which the continent might be found. The coasts discovered by these Dutchmen, however, all appeared unattractive and unpromising to the officials of a trading corporation, and the East India Company was unwilling to finance geographical exploration for its own sake. The systematic exploration of Australian waters was left to Cook and his successors, more than a century later.

One other incidental achievement of the Dutch company must be mentioned—the establishment of a colony at the Cape of Good Hope. This was the only true colony founded by the Dutch in the Old World in the seventeenth century. It was planted in 1652, not as

a trading station, but as a strategical support to the Indies commerce
and as a convenient halting place where the company's ships could
take in fuel, water and fresh provisions. The company, while retaining all freehold in its own hands, offered stock and leases on easy
terms and soon attracted a considerable number of settlers. Most of
these *boers* were peasants from Holland and elsewhere, who were
eager only for land and did not resent the political and commercial
restrictions placed upon them by the company. Within a few years
the colony was producing wine and provisions in considerable
quantities and had become a valuable asset. Politically it formed one
of the nine governments into which the Dutch Indies were divided,
under the general administrative supervision of Batavia; the others
being Ternate, Coromandel, Amboina, Banda, Ceylon, Malacca,
Macassar and the north-east coast of Java.

The most vivid illustration of the spread of European, and especially Dutch, sea power is to be found in the modifications of native
shipping in the Indian Ocean. European ships were not necessarily
more efficient than native ones for purposes of local trade, but Arab
and Indian owners soon found it prudent to make their ships as
European as possible in appearance. The *baghla* and the *ganja* acquired high transom sterns, carved and gilded in imitation of seven-
teenth- and eighteenth-century Indiamen. To this day some native
ships have dummy gunports painted along their sides. The Dutch
and the English established dock-yards in the East and introduced
European methods of fastening. Native builders began to produce
square-rigged types, notably the trim brigs and brigantines of the
Maldive Islands. Sailing ships still carry a great volume of trade in
the Indian Ocean, and many of the smaller ports are living museums,
full of small-scale models of the types of ship which fastened the
grip of European armed commerce on the Eastern seas in the
seventeenth century.

(ii) *Dutch rule in the islands*

Dutch colonial policy in the seventeenth century displayed little of
the careful stewardship which was to be its characteristic in later
times, and still less of the missionary paternalism and the care for
native rights which, officially at least, distinguished that of Spain.
Since the company acquired territory reluctantly, and only to make
its trade secure, it was unwilling to face the expense of any but a
purely commercial administration. The government at Batavia stood
at the head, not of a territory, but of a series of widely-scattered
establishments. Just as the company at Amsterdam was organised

as a firm of ship-owners of whom the governor-general was the paid agent, so the company's employees under the governor-general in the East held commercial, not administrative rank, as merchants, junior merchants, or clerks, though their actual work might be as directors of factories, commandants of forts or residents at the courts of native princes. At the elbow of the governor-general, and second only to him in importance, stood an executive officer known as the director-general of trade.

Although the company, as its activities expanded, could not avoid acquiring territory in the interests of its own safety, it could and did delegate the responsibilities of administration in those places where its possessions extended beyond port towns and the sites of factories. The immediate neighbourhood of Batavia was under direct Dutch rule; but in the other possessions of the company in Java, in Priangan and in the coastal areas, the duties of government were entrusted to regents, in theory the company's servants, in practice petty feudal lords, vassals of the company as they had formerly been vassals of Mataram. The regents had to obey the orders of the company's European officers; but as a rule the only orders they received concerned the delivery of produce for trade. In all other respects they ruled as petty local tyrants, very loosely supervised but sure of the company's support if their authority were resisted. Not until the eighteenth century did the company begin to appoint the subordinate officials of the regents and to pass their judicial decisions in review.

The more distant princes of Java in the late seventeenth century still boasted a more or less fictitious independence, ruling under the suzerainty or protection of the company, or in subordinate alliance with it. The senior Dutch officer at the court of each of these protected princes—the 'resident'—exercised both civil and criminal jurisdiction over the company's servants and other Europeans living in the principality. He administered Dutch law, with the local modifications contained in the statutes of Batavia. In respect of the native princes and their subjects, the functions of the 'residents' were primarily commercial. Interference with native justice was exceptional. Non-European foreigners, of whom the Chinese were by far the most numerous, lived under the jurisdiction of their own headmen in accordance with the normal custom throughout the East. Outside Java, the same gradations of Dutch rule, direct and indirect, existed. Except for port towns and factories, only the small but important spice-producing areas of Amboina and the Banda Islands were administered directly by the company. In Ternate, in Macassar, and elsewhere, Dutch interests were protected as in Java, by treaties of alliance or protectorate enforced by Dutch 'residents'.

The company derived its revenue, in the first instance, from the profits of trading; but since its trade was a jealously guarded monopoly, it began, as soon as its growing power permitted, to regulate production in order to maintain prices, and to confine the production of especially valuable crops to areas under its own control. It sought to achieve these ends in its own territory by direct administrative action, and elsewhere by the treaties which it imposed upon defeated native rulers. From the regulation of production, to the levy of tribute in kind under colour of trade, was but a short step. The principal duty of the regents in occupied Java was to supply to the company, free of cost, fixed quantities of pepper, indigo and cotton-yarn. The treaty with the *Susuhunan* of Mataram in 1677–8 required that prince to deliver annual consignments of rice at a fixed price; and the Sultan of Bantam by a similar treaty was compelled to sell to the company, at its own price, the whole pepper crop of his kingdom. In theory a distinction was maintained between 'contingencies', which were undisguised tributes in kind, and 'forced deliveries', trading contracts exceptionally favourable to the purchaser; but in practice these two sources of revenue, which came to form the bulk of the company's income, were confused both with one another and with the proceeds of ordinary trade. Compared with these tributes, open and disguised, taxation in the ordinary sense was unimportant. As a rule only Europeans paid direct taxes in money, and Europeans were the chief contributors under most heads of indirect taxation; but natives under Dutch rule were liable to forced labour, particularly for harbour works. The Batavia Dutch, with grim humour, applied the name 'Mud Javanese' to the native gangs recruited for the work of dredging Batavia harbour. In the Banda Islands the Dutch resorted to slave labour for the cultivation of spices, after the extirpation of the native population.

The production of spices was naturally the economic activity most rigorously controlled by the company in the seventeenth century. The treaty of 1657 with the Sultan of Ternate had confined spice-growing in the Moluccas to islands directly controlled by the Dutch. In those islands, production was ruthlessly adjusted to trade needs year by year. In some years, trees were cut down to avoid a surplus; in others, the inhabitants were compelled to plant trees at the expense of other crops. In addition to this economic uncertainty, the policy of economic strangulation applied by the Dutch to weaken the power of Mataram deprived the spice islands of their source of rice and reduced their people to an inadequate diet of sago. A chronic state of semi-starvation ensued. The manipulation of spice production continued until the second half of the eighteenth

century, by which time the French and English, by growing spices
in their own possessions, had broken the Dutch monopoly. Meanwhile, coffee had appeared as another valuable and easily manipu-
lated crop. Coffee had first been imported into Holland from Mocha
in 1661, and was introduced into the East Indies at the end of the
century. The first consignment of Java coffee was shipped to Holland
in 1712. Grown under compulsion, it became in the eighteenth century the most important product of the Dutch East Indies.

The Dutch monopoly of the spice trade, and the policy by which
it was maintained, produced desolation and permanent decline in
the Moluccas and parts of Celebes. Elsewhere, however, and particularly in Java, although native social and economic life suffered
in many ways, the blame cannot be laid entirely upon the Dutch. The
Muslim conquest of the early sixteenth century had already under-
mined Hindu-Javanese civilisation. Portuguese intervention in the
trade between the spice islands and Malacca had side-tracked Javanese commerce. The Dutch merely completed what others had begun. In order to break the power of the *Susuhunan* of Mataram,
they set themselves to destroy trade and all intercourse between
Mataram and the outside world. This policy they pursued with
great energy and success. Traders and ship-builders lost their occupations and the Javanese became almost entirely a race of cultivators;
the only customer for their crops being the Dutch company. The
rice export of Java suffered most severely. On the other hand, the
Dutch encouraged and increased the production of sugar—grown
mainly on Chinese estates—and indigo; they introduced new crops
—coffee, agave, ground-nuts; their interest in trade and production
made them, on the whole, effective supporters of political stability.
In the eighteenth century, Java, run by the company as a vast estate,
began to make visible economic progress once again; and as population increased, even the abandoned rice-fields came back into cultivation.

In social life, discrimination against Asiatics as such was unknown either in law or in practice, and mixed marriages were common; though the company was at pains to prevent half-castes and
non-Europeans going to Holland. There was sharp discrimination
in law against non-Christians. In Batavia the public exercise of any
worship except that of the Dutch Reformed Church was forbidden.
In practice, despite the protests of the ministers, Hindus, Muslims
and Chinese enjoyed complete freedom of worship immediately
outside the walls and—as far as the company was concerned—
elsewhere in the Indies. Like most Protestant Europeans at that time,
the Dutch showed comparatively little interest in missionary work.

The great variety of Malayan dialects, moreover, made systematic preaching among the natives impossible. Throughout the seventeenth century Portuguese remained the chief *lingua franca* of the archipelago; and the few native converts to Calvinism came mostly from among Portuguese-speaking Catholics.

In sharp contrast, Islam under Dutch pressure displayed a great and increasing vitality. Behind the moral force of Muslim preaching lay the political force of the empires of Turkey, of Persia and of north India. From time to time the Indonesian princes, in particular the *Susuhunan,* tried to arouse the interest and sympathy of these mighty states in the affairs of the Far Eastern Muslims. Had they succeeded, considerable damage might have been done to European interests in the Near and Middle East. The attempts failed; but even so, the hold of Islam upon the Indonesian peoples grew stronger, not weaker, in all the settled regions except Bali. Apart from the Hindus of Bali, the only Asiatics in the archipelago who remained unaffected were the Chinese, whose numbers and whose influence increased steadily under Dutch rule and have continued to increase ever since. In general, the influence of the Dutch invasion, irresistible in commerce and powerful in politics, was much weaker in ordinary social life, and in religious affairs almost negligible.

(iii) *Rival powers in India*

The English East India Company's factory at Surat, established with the permission of the local Mughal governor, enjoyed a long and on the whole prosperous career as a depot for cotton, muslin, saltpetre and indigo from the interior of north India. Naturally the ubiquitous Dutch soon appeared to claim a share of the trade; but they could not evict the English by force, nor could the English evict them. A breach of the peace within the Mughal dominions at that time would have led to the eviction of both parties. For the Dutch the trade of the Indian mainland was secondary to the more lucrative trade with the East Indies, and the high-handed methods which they habitually employed against the Indonesian princes would have been mere impertinence in dealing with the Mughal empire. The English, humble through knowledge of their relative weakness, held the trade of Surat against all European rivals. The occasional misfortunes which they suffered were the results either of local famines or of temporary losses of Mughal favour. They were blamed and punished in 1623 for piracies committed by the Dutch against pilgrim ships plying to Mecca; and again in 1636 for the

similar piracies of English captains, authorised by Charles I to visit
India in contravention of the company's charter. Apart from these
interludes the factors at Surat drove a profitable and peaceful trade
as long as the Mughal power protected them; and the company's
ships made some small return by policing the pilgrim route and by
privateering against Dutch and Portuguese, under letters of marque
from the Emperor.

In south-east India Dutch competition was more formidable. The
Coromandel coast was more easily accessible for a trade in 'white
cloth' with the Dutch headquarters in Java. The local rulers on the
coast—vassals either of the Muslim kings of Golconda or of the
Hindu successors of once great Vijayanagar—were less powerful
and less dependable than the Mughal viceroys. The English at
Masulipatam and the Dutch at Pulicat, enjoying the favour of different princes, competed and occasionally fought with one another
throughout the century. On the whole, the English fared better than
the Dutch at the game of Indian politics, largely because of their
persistence in securing the protection of great overlords such as the
Mughal Emperor or the King of Golconda, instead of relying upon
agreements with the petty rajas of the coast. From 1634 the policy of
the English company was to maintain a 'Continual Residence' at
the Golconda court.

In 1639 Francis Day, factor at Masulipatam, turned the flank
of the Dutch by founding a factory at Madras and by securing—
despite opposition from his directors—permission from the local
raja to build a fort. The Madras grant included not only the factory site, but about six square miles of territory along the coast,
including the old Portuguese mission of St Thomas's Mount.
This was the first English acquisition of territory in India. The
directors complained bitterly of the expense of fortification and of
maintaining a garrison of a hundred men; but the advancement of
the company's interests always owed more to individual initiative
in India than to the inspiration and support of London. Day's plans
went forward on the strength of the approval of the company's
officers in India, and Madras grew steadily in importance from its
first foundation. The worst enemy of the India trade was famine,
and famine visited Madras in 1647; but the factory and garrison
were saved from starvation in the midst of a starving country by
provisions shipped from Surat—a display of power and resource
which so impressed the King of Golconda that he became more
than ever the company's friend. He had already, in 1645, confirmed
the Madras grant. Gradually the directors in London became aware
of the trade possibilities in the Bay of Bengal. In 1658 the company,

strengthened and encouraged by Cromwell's charter of the year before, made Madras its headquarters for eastern India.

1658 was the year of the accession of Aurangzeb, the last great Mughal emperor; a grim and earnest Muslim fanatic. Throughout the first half of the seventeenth century the policy and practice of the English company, as far as the Indians were concerned, was peaceful, unarmed trade. Its resources were at first too small to support a more aggressive policy. It relied upon the great Indian powers for protection, not only against banditry, but to some extent against the intrusion of other Europeans on land. On the high seas its ships could look after themselves. But an armed monopoly was the implied object of the English company, as of most European trading companies, and changes in the political situation in India eventually brought about an overt change in the company's policy. Aurangzeb's religious persecution alienated the Rajput princes, in Akbar's time the strongest supporters of the empire, and provoked widespread risings among Hindus from the Punjab to the Deccan. The military efficiency of the empire, no longer reinforced by immigrants from central Asia, was declining. In central India a predatory Hindu power, the Maratha confederacy, raided the Mughal provinces and through years of guerrilla warfare resisted or evaded the unwieldy imperial armies.

In 1664 the Marathas raided Surat. They sacked the town but were beaten off by the company's men from the walls of the English factory. For the first time the Mughal had failed to protect his clients, and the company began to look round for means to defend itself. The first requirement was a defensible base, if possible outside the imperial jurisdiction; and such a base lay ready to hand. Bombay had come into Charles II's hands as part of Catherine of Braganza's dowry. His ships had taken possession in 1665, after a protracted dispute with the resident Portuguese, and in 1668, finding the town an expensive liability, he had leased it to the company. It was pestilent but readily defensible, and from 1669 Aungier, the president at Surat, began the work of developing and fortifying the harbour. He established a gunboat squadron as a protection against local pirates and boldly entered into treaty relations with Sivaji, the Maratha chieftain upon whose flank he was entrenched. By 1677, the year of Aungier's death, the trade of Bombay already rivalled that of Surat. The old dependence upon Mughal favour was broken and the company had embarked upon a career of trading sword in hand.

The same growing forces of disorder which had threatened Surat afflicted eastern India also. Madras was threatened by Sivaji in 1677, and a few years later by Aurangzeb himself in the course of his southern campaigns. In Bengal, the small and struggling English factories protested vainly against the exactions of a semi-independent Mughal viceroy, until another local leader, Job Charnock, established a defensible base at Calcutta in the swamps of the Ganges delta. That was in 1686; by that time Charnock's quarrel with the viceroy in Bengal had widened into a general war against the Mughal empire. The policy of unarmed trade had been abandoned and the company was looking to its servants 'to establish such a policy of civil and military power, and create and secure such a large revenue as may be the foundation of a large, well-grounded, sure English dominion in India for all time to come'. This change of policy was made in conscious imitation of the Dutch; but only ignorance of the forces and the distances involved could have impelled the company to declare war and to send a puny expedition of a few hundred men against an empire which maintained in the field an army of at least a hundred thousand. The English declaration of war, however, if it ever reached Aurangzeb, was for him a matter of small importance; the Emperor was away in south India, fighting the campaigns which destroyed the states of Golconda and Bijapur, but which left intact the real enemy, the power of the Marathas. It was only the company's depredations by sea on the route to Mecca which drew Aurangzeb's attention to this minor war. His officers accordingly seized the company's factories at Surat and Masulipatam and cast its agents into prison. Probably only an appreciation of the English power at sea and the consequent threat to the pilgrim route saved the factors from complete expulsion. As it was, the company sued for peace, and in 1690 obtained a fresh licence to trade at the cost of humble submission and a heavy fine. In the same year Calcutta, abandoned during the war, was reoccupied, this time permanently, and the first buildings of a great city began to appear on the fever-ridden banks of the Ganges.

Although the Mughal empire was still too strong for the English on land, its power was fast declining. Aurangzeb's reign saw the greatest territorial extension of the Mughal power, and the beginning of its disintegration. During his long absence in south India, he lost much of his control over Delhi and the north. His *subadars* became semi-independent feudatories, and his last twenty-five years were a weary and losing battle against growing anarchy. He died in 1707. Under the feeble rule of his successors not only the Mughal viceroys, but Muslim adventurers great and small, some within India and some invaders from Persia and Afghanistan carved out independent principalities with their swords. Many of these ephemeral kingdoms were in their turn destroyed by the Marathas, who year by year extended the area of their plundering raids. In the anarchy which ensued, peaceful unarmed trade became impossible. The Marathas paved the way for European political intervention in defence of commercial monopolies. The same train of events which had turned Aurangzeb into a wandering soldier, drove the English company in the eighteenth century to political intrigue and military adventure. From being a mere commercial undertaking it was to become a territorial overlord and a gatherer of tribute on a vast scale.

During all the vicissitudes of the later seventeenth century the company's commerce flourished. Its misfortunes were mainly local ones. While one factory was in trouble another showed a handsome profit. The profits of the company were still made chiefly by exporting bullion, purchasing Eastern goods, and selling them in Europe. It exported woollens at a loss, as a concession to mercantile opinion and to conciliate the manufacturing interest; English manufactured goods did not command a ready sale in India until the late eighteenth century. Nevertheless, during the period 1657–91 the average annual dividend was about twenty-five per cent, and in 1683—the peak year—the company's hundred pound shares were being sold for five hundred pounds. Naturally in a period of mounting prosperity the company found increasing difficulty in maintaining its monopoly; the concessions which it made—the opening of the port-to-port trade in India, and the licences granted to ten or twelve 'permission ships' to clear for India from England each year—were inadequate to meet the demands of the wealthier interlopers. While the Stuart kings ruled, the danger was small, for Charles II and James II were both shareholders and staunch supporters of the company; but under William III, the fact that the company held a royal and not a parliamentary charter was made the ground of a legal onslaught by the interlopers. In India the company was strong enough to protect itself and to capture many interloping ships; but in London its constitutional position was weakened by the Revolution; and the interlopers soon learned the value of corporate action. They formed themselves into an association in 1690, and began to petition Parliament to throw open the Indian trade. Eventually in 1698 they obtained an Act incorporating them as the New (or English, as distinct from London) East India Company, on condition of a loan of £2,000,000 to the government. The Old Company duly received notice of the termination of its charter; but its members retrieved their parliamentary defeat by subscribing largely to the new loan and so securing a considerable share of the privileges of the New Company. There followed ten years of struggle and competitive bribery. In India the Old Company had all the advantages of established factories and experienced agents and in 1702 its charter was prolonged for a further seven years. By that time the schism and the political struggle were involving both parties in ruinous expense. Finally in 1708–9 the two companies amalgamated. The United Company of Merchants of England trading to the East Indies entered upon a long period of steady advance as a powerful armed monopoly, almost undisturbed by faction at home. In 1715, it opened a new chapter in its history, in a regular trade with China, and Chinese tea eventually became the most important of the commodities which it brought to England.

The principal challenge to the growing power of the company in the eighteenth century was to come from other European rivals. The Dutch, it is true, in the face of growing difficulties in India, tended to withdraw more and more to the archipelago where their dominance was now undisputed. The Portuguese retained their capital at Goa, but their power at sea was only a fraction of what it had once been. The Danes, with a modest factory at Tranquebar, concerned themselves mainly with the China trade and were never dangerous competitors. The chief rivals of the English were the French. Colbert's East India Company of 1664, after a promising beginning, had existed precariously through the long wars against the Dutch and the English in Europe and America. Its main enemy was unsound finance; between 1688 and 1713 there was little fighting between English and French in India, for neither side felt strong enough to risk a struggle in the presence of formidable native powers. After the death of Aurangzeb this deterrent was removed. Much of the history of India in the eighteenth century is the story of the naval and political struggle between French and English for commercial mastery. The French, with their single headquarters at Pondicherry, had the advantage of good relations with the native princes, and possessed the skill and tact to maintain those relations. The advantage of the English lay in first-class bases— Bombay, Madras, Calcutta—in widely separated regions. Ultimately the struggle was decided by the ability of the English to cut communications between France and India by the use of force at sea.

SLAVERY AND THE WAR FOR TRADE

(i) *Slavery in Spanish America*

The most valuable products of the American colonies, sugar, tobacco and, later, cotton, were cultivated by processes requiring comparatively little skill. What they did require was an abundance of virgin soil, so that when a piece of land had been exhausted, a fresh piece could be taken in. They required also a great army of unskilled labour, which could be kept for long hours at monotonous work in a climate in which the white man, though he can work if he must, prefers not to. All the colonies suffered from a chronic shortage of labour. The various free racial groups, white, Indian and half-caste, were in some colonies too few in number to supply the need. In other places, though numerous, they were unwilling to do plantation work and for various reasons were difficult to coerce. In Spanish America, for instance, the Spaniards were too proud or too lazy. The Indians were too indifferent to wages and too sensitive to loss of liberty. They enjoyed legal protection against enslavement, and *repartimiento* gangs were too temporary and uncertain for the continuous labour of the sugar plantations. The *mestizos* inherited the characteristics of one or other of their parents. They, too, made poor labourers. Negro slaves supplied the obvious solution.

The import of Africans to replace the dwindling native population of the Antilles began in the very first years of the sixteenth century. It was carried on under crown licence, and although some Dominicans had misgivings about it, there was no serious opposition from the missionary Orders in general. It seems curious at first sight that the Spanish Crown, always so emphatic about the personal freedom of Indians, should see nothing inconsistent in Negro slavery; but to the sixteenth- or seventeenth-century mind the two cases were widely different. The objections to the enslavement of Indians were primarily legal ones. The Indians were subjects of the Crown of Castille and were entitled to protection. Negroes, on the other hand, were the subjects of independent kings. Europeans visited West Africa as traders, not as over-lords. If the local rulers made war among themselves and sold their prisoners to Arab or European slave dealers, that was not the fault of the King of Spain. The enslavement of prisoners of war was a normal proceeding in many parts of the world. The theorists laid down that the war must be a just war; but obviously in practice it was impossible for the purchasers of slaves to form a judgment on that point. In any case the Negro was widely regarded as a superior animal, physically much better fitted for hard work than the Indian.

Slavery was a familiar institution in sixteenth-century Europe, and especially common in southern Europe. The Portuguese connection with North and West Africa had made the Negro slave a familiar figure in Portugal and Spain long before the discovery of America. In the Moorish wars and the constant fighting against the corsair towns on the Barbary coast, prisoners were regularly enslaved on both sides, and all the naval powers of the Mediterranean employed slaves to row their galleys. Household slavery survived into the eighteenth century. As for the trade in slaves for general labour, the discovery of America gave it a new lease of life, and until the late eighteenth century no serious doubts were cast upon its legitimacy.

For the Spaniards, the main difficulty was the practical one of obtaining a steady supply of slaves. Apart from ill-treatment and overwork, many Negroes died in epidemics of unfamiliar diseases and as a result of drinking raw spirits in the sugar plantations. From the owners' point of view, replacement was more economical than rearing slave children. More and more Negroes were constantly required and the Spanish commercial system could not supply them in sufficient quantity.

Except for a few years under Charles V, the slave-trade with the Indies was confined to the ports of Seville and Cadiz, and officially only Castillian subjects who were members of the Seville *consulado* might engage in it. Other persons required special licence. From an early date the Crown began to sell special licences to slave-traders shipping to America; but it still endeavoured to compel slave ships to sail from Seville, for two principal reasons: one, to enforce the payment of export duty, the other, to ensure that all slaves shipped to the Indies were genuine Guinea Negroes and not slaves of Muslim religion from North Africa, who might corrupt the Indians. Spaniards, however, had no lawful access to the West African coast; nor had Portuguese merchants lawful access to the Spanish Indies. Spanish slavers clearing from Seville had therefore to buy their slaves through Portuguese middlemen. All these charges, inconveniences and delays added to the mortality of the slaves on passage and to their price when they arrived. The only concession the Crown would make was to allow slavers to sail independently instead of waiting for the regular convoys.

One experiment was made in the first half of the sixteenth century in contracting for the supply of slaves in bulk. In 1528 a German merchant and banker named Ehinger contracted to supply four thousand slaves to the Indies in four years. The Crown in return undertook to issue no other licences during that period, so that Ehinger was in effect granted a monopoly of the trade. Ehinger, however, in order to fulfil his contract in the stated time, let out large numbers of his licences to sub-contractors, many of whom were Portuguese, and these sub-contractors appointed factors to reside in Spanish American ports to retail the slaves. This arrangement suited the Spanish colonists admirably, but alarmed the Spanish government. Ehinger's contract was not renewed and the Portuguese factors were expelled. The Portuguese undoubtedly continued to smuggle a certain number of slaves, especially to Venezuela where the demand was strongest; but as the Brazilian sugar industry developed and itself demanded slaves, the traders had less inducement to carry their cargoes to the Spanish Indies in defiance of the authorities. The Spanish licence system never succeeded in supplying slaves in anything like the required numbers. When in the fifteen-sixties Sir John Hawkins began his series of slaving voyages, buying slaves on the Guinea coast and shipping them direct to the Indies, he found a ready market and was able, moreover, to undersell the licensed slavers wherever he went.

The union of the Spanish and Portuguese crowns in 1580 presented the Spanish government with a solution of its slaving problem. Without violating its own commercial laws it could make use of the experience and facilities possessed by the Portuguese. The Portuguese possessed slaving stations on the Guinea coast and ships to carry the slaves; in their connections with local dealers they also possessed the good-will of the business—if the word good-will can be used of this appalling trade. For the first fifteen years of the union of the crowns the Spanish government continued to sell individual licences as before, but many, probably most of these licences were sold to Portuguese traders, and the number of Negroes in the sugar-

producing areas of the Spanish Main mounted rapidly. The rest of
the trade of Spanish America remained closed to all except Castil-
lians. Participation in the Spanish slave trade was the only compen-
sation the Portuguese received for the loss of national independence
and for the disasters which befell their empire under Spanish rule.

(ii) *Slavery in the Sugar Islands*

Throughout the sixteenth and seventeenth centuries the slave trade
was the handmaid of the sugar industry. The Negroes whom Sir
John Hawkins shipped to the Caribbean with so large a profit to
himself were mostly destined to work on Spanish sugar plantations.
When Hawkins was driven off by the Spaniards the English temporarily dropped out of the slave trade, leaving it to the Portuguese;
but in the seventeenth century Portuguese trade under Spanish rule
began to decline, and much of it was lost to the Dutch West India
Company and to the numerous Dutch private interlopers. The Dutch
themselves established sugar plantations in Guiana and northern
Brazil and undertook the supply of slaves. Soon they began to oust
the Portuguese from most of their factories on the Slave Coast. The
great fort at Elmina fell to the Dutch in 1637, and the easy-going
Portuguese suzerainty of a native town was replaced by the more
efficient but also more grasping administration of a commercial
company. The newcomers, by local alliances and the use of native
mercenaries, quickly secured themselves against the competition of
other Europeans seeking to trade on that part of the Coast.

In 1640, when the Dutch ascendancy was at its height, the cultivation of sugar was introduced into Barbados, and the English
planters began to demand slaves in their turn. They were supplied
throughout the Civil War and Commonwealth period by the Dutch
slavers; but after the Restoration this trade naturally came in for
adverse comment in England. It was contrary to mercantile policy
to buy so valuable a commodity from foreigners, and the Navigation
Acts had made it illegal for Dutch ships to trade to English colonies.
An alternative method of supply had to be found, and the only possible method was to establish a monopolistic company. An open
trade would have been impossible, in face of the inevitable hostility
of the Dutch, firmly entrenched on the Slave Coast. The English
Crown had not the resources to undertake the building of forts and
the provision of armed ships, so a company had to be formed
for the purpose, and in 1660, the first year of the restored monarchy,
Charles II granted a charter to the concern which later became

known as the Royal Africa Company. The King himself was a shareholder. The intention was to supply the English sugar colonies with three thousand slaves a year at an average price of £17, or one ton of sugar, per slave.

Through its many financial and constitutional vicissitudes the company drove a thriving trade, but nevertheless was perpetually on the verge of bankruptcy. There were three main reasons for this —the same difficulties which afflicted nearly all the great trading companies. One was the constant interruption of commerce by war, in this case the Dutch wars, which involved the company in serious losses of forts and ships and soon compelled it to put up its price to £25 or £35 per slave. As soon as the company had established itself on the Slave Coast, moreover, its monopoly was invaded by the inevitable interlopers, who took advantage of the company's arrangements with the slave-dealing chiefs and proceeded to undersell the company in the West Indies. Thirdly, the company, like all such concerns, was cheated by its own agents, who bought slaves on their own account, transported them in the company's ships, and sold them privately at the other end. This practice led to appalling overcrowding and a very high mortality on passage. The losses fell, of course, on the company; the Negroes who died were always the company's slaves.

The company could increase its profits by selling some of its slaves at an enhanced price to the Spanish colonies; but Spanish American ports were still legally closed to English shipping. One solution of this difficulty was to make the Spaniards come to Jamaica or Barbados, buy their slaves there and take them away in their own ships; but that was contrary to the Navigation Act. The company had recourse, therefore, to one of the powers of the royal prerogative which was beginning to be a subject of constitutional dispute—the power to grant dispensations from statutes in particular cases. In 1663, Charles II granted a dispensation from the Navigation Act, to allow Spanish ships to visit English West Indian harbours for the purpose of buying slaves. The company sold a number of slaves to Spaniards in this way in Barbados; but the innovation raised a storm of protest among the English West Indian planters. They wanted all the available slaves for their own plantations. They feared that the competition of Spanish buyers would raise the price, and that the slaves sold to the Spaniards would be employed in producing sugar, which would compete with their own sugar in the European market. They carried on a bitter propaganda campaign against the Royal Africa Company's monopoly, clamoured constantly for a free trade in slaves, and continued to buy slaves from interlopers whenever they could.

Official mercantilist policy towards the slave trade faced a fundamental dilemma. Was the trade merely a means to an end, to supply the English colonies with slaves in order to increase and cheapen the production of sugar? Or was it to be an end in itself, to supply slaves to any market, English or foreign, where a demand existed? The Royal Africa Company was a very influential corporation, and probably the government's decisions were affected by other considerations than pure economic theory. In the late seventeenth century the government on the whole supported the claims of the slavers against those of the planters. It appeared, however, that the only hope of pleasing everybody lay in securing a separate contract for the supply of slaves to Spanish America—such a contract as the French succeeded in obtaining in 1701, to the general English dismay.

These disputes about the slave trade were almost unaffected by moral or humanitarian considerations. Sailors disliked shipping in slave ships, and a few Quakers protested against the trade on moral grounds; but the references to it in business correspondence contain no indication that a trade in human beings differed radically from a trade in any other commodity. No social stigma attached to it. Its legality rested on the independence of the native African kings who supplied the slaves. The victims were slaves before the traders bought them. Kidnapping being, it was claimed, a recognised custom of the African people and authorised by their kings, it was covered by a veneer of African constitutionalism. Slavery itself in the eighteenth century was justified legally by a somewhat forced analogy with English villeinage; Lord Chancellor Hardwicke holding that though villein tenures were extinct in practice, no positive law had ever abolished the status of villeinage. A similar argument was used in France, where serfdom was by no means extinct. In the English colonies no common law justification was required for slavery, since in most places it was defined and legalised by positive laws enacted by colonial assemblies. The French colonies possessed a general code of slave law, the *Code Noir*, established by Louis XIV in 1685, guaranteeing to slaves a number of important civil rights and prohibiting the separation of families. The Spanish laws of the Indies contained similar provisions, and on the whole Negro slaves seem to have been better treated in the Spanish dependencies than elsewhere; but in practice the plantation slave everywhere was very much at the mercy of his owner.

The slave trade naturally had far-reaching effects upon the

population of the Americas. In Spanish and Portuguese America slave labour was more or less confined to sugar-growing areas and was not much employed in the production of tobacco; but in the English and French empires slaves were widely used in producing tobacco, rice and later cotton. Slavery has its own Gresham's law. Slave labour drives out free labour, and slave plantations drive out yeoman farmers. It is not simply a matter of colour, though that, of course, is a contributory factor. In most of the West Indian islands the white population began to dwindle as soon as sugar was introduced. In the eighteenth century the white population of Jamaica sank to 7 per cent of the whole, that of Antigua to 6 per cent. In Barbados, the white farmers, settled before the introduction of sugar, proved more tenacious. Barbados also continued to attract indented servants, who often became overseers; but even so, the white proportion in Barbados at the end of the eighteenth century was only 26 per cent. Northern Brazil is partly populated by Negroes for the same reasons, Haiti is a Negro republic, Santo Domingo largely Negro. In Mexico the Negro is comparatively unimportant, because the Indians are numerous and sugar a less important crop. In Virginia and the Carolinas, white farmers were driven away from the big plantation areas near the coast. The slave planter, as they used to say in the southern States, is a land-killer; in all the places where the slavers drove their briskest trade, they left a legacy of exhausted land and a mass of discontented freedmen to be provided for. Yet seventeenth- and eighteenth-century statesmen had no inkling of all this. They saw merely that the slave trade had enriched the Portuguese in the sixteenth century, the Dutch in the seventeenth. The maritime powers struggled for a share in the slave trade as assiduously as ever they fought for the possession of colonial territory.

(iii) *The* Asientos

Spanish America in the sixteenth century depended largely upon the Portuguese, as we have seen, for its supply of slaves. In 1595 the Spanish government, accepting the inevitable, consented to the first of a long series of slave *Asientos*. This was an agreement for farming out the slave trade, or the greater part of it, to a contractor who was to organise the whole business, maintaining his own stations in Spain, in Africa and in the Indies. He was to take over from the government the task of selling licences to sub-contractors, remitting the licence fees to the Crown. He and his sub-contractors might ship slaves directly from Africa to America, making their own arrange-

ments for convoy and escort if necessary. The port of Buenos Aires
was temporarily opened for the reception of slaves. This was a great
concession, for owing to the difficulty of controlling the trade of
Buenos Aires the Crown had for many years kept the port closed to
all trade. In return for this concession the contractor undertook to
ship certain quantities of slaves to ports designated by the Crown,
where slaves were urgently needed.

The first *Asiento* was granted to a Portuguese contractor named
Reynel. He undertook to supply 38,000 slaves to the Indies in nine
years. The form of his agreement was used for subsequent *Asientos*
down to 1640. In the early seventeenth century vast numbers of
slaves were shipped over in Portuguese ships and both the Crown
and the contractors had every reason to be satisfied with the arrangement. The group of Lisbon merchants engaged in the slave
trade were, indeed, almost the only Portuguese who wished to
remain under Spanish government. From the sixteen-twenties, however, the effects of Dutch competition began to be felt, the Portuguese contractors found it increasingly difficult to obtain cargoes in
Africa and were compelled to raise their prices. Finally, in 1640,
Portugal revolted successfully against Spanish rule and the *Asiento*
broke down.

The Spanish Crown tried at once to revert to the system of individual licences as it had existed before 1580; but times had changed.
The Dutch had seized Curaçao in 1634. The English, expelled from
Providence Island in 1641, took Jamaica in 1655. The commercial
enemies of Spain, therefore, had trading stations on the very thresh-
old of the Indies. The slave trade had become too unprofitable and
too dangerous for Spaniards, even if they could obtain the Negroes.
A slaver, with his highly perishable cargo, could not afford to wait
about in the Seville river for convoys; and for an independent
Spanish ship to sail unescorted through a Caribbean full of buccaneers was a perilous enterprise. The Spanish government's licences
found very few takers. From 1640 to the end of the seventeenth
century the slave trade to the Spanish Indies was mainly contraband
in Dutch or English hands. With the slave trade went an equally
lucrative illicit trade in the main products of the Indies, especially
sugar, tobacco, cacao and silver. The Spanish trade monopoly, therefore, never very complete in practice, during this period broke down
almost entirely.

The *Asiento* offered a means whereby the Spanish government
could regain at least a measure of indirect control over the slave
trade with its own colonies, on the assumption that a contractor, if
granted a monopoly, would do something to protect the monopoly

against the English and the Dutch. There were now, however, no servants of the Spanish crown able to undertake so large an enterprise. The *Asiento*, if revived at all, would have to go to a foreign company; and it was now regarded as so valuable a concession that its grant necessarily acquired all the characteristics of an international treaty. The Spaniards put their pride in their pockets and negotiated brief arrangements first with a Genoese company, then (a bitter humiliation) with a Portuguese, both of whom partly fulfilled their contracts with the assistance of English and Dutch subcontractors. Neither *Asiento* proved satisfactory. Finally, at the end of the century, a solution appeared which was both acceptable to Spanish pride and equal to the needs of the situation. The French, during the second half of the seventeenth century, had begun to take a close interest in the West African coast and had established factories in Senegal. A union between the Spanish and French Crowns, or at least a Bourbon prince on the Spanish throne, seemed at the end of the century to be a likely development; and no more suitable contractor for the *Asiento* could be found. An *Asiento* was accordingly concluded with the French Guinea Company in 1701. The French had a trade plan very similar to that of the English. Like the English, they possessed sugar-producing islands—Guadeloupe, Martinique and Grenade; and they had lately, by the treaty of Ryswyck in 1697, secured from Spain the western half of Hispaniola, which later became the Negro republic of Haiti. The French Guinea Company proposed to monopolise the supply of slaves both to their own islands and to the Spanish possessions.

This arrangement naturally did not suit the English or the Dutch; and while no doubt the principal concern of the English in the war of the Spanish Succession was to keep Louis XIV and his relatives off the throne of Spain, the Netherlands and the Indies, at least a subsidiary motive was to prevent the French Guinea Company from keeping the slave *Asiento*. This object was, of course, achieved. The Spanish government was persuaded or bullied into cancelling the French agreement and at the end of the war the *Asiento* was granted to an English company, the South Sea Company, formed for the purpose, which was to buy slaves from the Royal Africa Company and retail them at the Spanish American ports.

With the *Asiento* went the right accorded to the South Sea Company to send a ship-load of general merchandise every year to Portobello fair—the first acknowledged exception to the Spanish trade monopoly, an exception grudgingly made and rigidly limited. The annual ship was of no great material importance in itself. Only eight ships were in fact sent to Portobello, and the story of the trade is one of obstruction on the Spanish side and fraud on the English—of ships replenishing their cargoes from pinnaces at night, and of naval escorts freighted with illicit merchandise. The Spaniards, in consequence, did their best to end the trade and eventually succeeded. The company was of course fantastically over-capitalised for the amount of business open to it, and feverish attempts to extend its general trade ended in a disastrous financial failure.

The *Asiento*, on the other hand, was still regarded as a valuable concession, not merely on account of the slave trade, but also on account of the facilities it offered for the carriage of contraband of all kinds. Even in slaving the company made little or no profit; but the interlopers who followed in its wake often made large fortunes. The English after nearly two hundred years of smuggling and buccaneering had at last collected a great part of the commerce of the Spanish empire into their own hands, and had done so through the medium of the slave trade. It is not surprising that the trade received official blessing in England. The slaving agreement with Spain lasted without a break until 1739, when it was interrupted by another war, occasioned by trading disputes—the 'war of Jenkins's ear'. The slave *Asiento* was finally surrendered in 1750, the Spanish Crown compensating the English company by a cash payment of £100,000. By that time the English were firmly established as the slave traders in chief to all the Americas.

(iv) *The Spanish Succession*

The commercial concessions secured by the victors in the war of the Spanish Succession fell far short of their original hopes, the Spanish government proving more obstinate than was expected. Nor did the enemies of France succeed in driving Louis XIV's grandson from the throne of Spain. By the end of the war, however, it had become clear that there was no real danger of French control of the Spanish Indies; and as for the Spanish Netherlands, the peace treaty itself detached them from Spain. The treaty of Utrecht, in general, was a classic example of international compromise. In the colonial field, however, it sanctioned a number of important changes of territorial possession, which were to prove permanent.

French North America was dismembered. Nova Scotia—Acadia —had for a century been the object of attack from the south, and its towns had been captured over and over again by the English or the New Englanders, only to be restored. Now the treaty of Utrecht assigned to England not only Nova Scotia (with an undefined inland boundary) but the whole of Newfoundland; though French fishermen retained the right to use the western shore. Cape Breton Island remained French, and on it the French proceeded to build their most impressive colonial fortress, Louisbourg; a bold threat to English security in that region, though, without the sea power to back it, an empty threat, as events later proved.

The shores of Hudson's Bay, with the fortresses which the French had built or captured there, were confirmed to England. The definition of the land boundary between Rupert's Land—the Hudson's Bay Company's territory—and Canada, was left to a commission, which eventually agreed upon latitude 49°N.—the parallel which now forms the northern frontier of the United States west of the Great Lakes. French Canada was hemmed in on the north and north-west by the company's territory, on the south and east by New York, New England and Nova Scotia. The only route still open for French-Canadian expansion was south-west down the Mississippi towards the junction with Louisiana. New Orleans, the capital of Louisiana, was established as a permanent settlement in 1717.

In the West Indies, the territorial changes of the treaty of Utrecht were unimportant. England obtained the whole of St Kitt's for the first time, but France retained the much more valuable colony of St Domingue, first secured in the treaty of Ryswyck. Although the English sugar islands were beginning to show the effects of soil exhaustion, and the larger French islands were not, yet the English West Indian planters maintained a firm and successful opposition to any English project for acquiring new islands, whose sugar might compete with their own. The old dilemma of the English slave-traders thus persisted; whether to sell slaves, for present profit, to foreign sugar growers? The French islands competed more and more successfully in the eighteenth century, both in buying slaves and in selling sugar. One of the results was the unhappy story of the molasses legislation; a combination of exasperation and futility.

The losses of Spain were all in Europe—the Netherlands, Minorca and—small but significant loss—Gibraltar, which an English fleet had seized in 1704. In America, despite a small legal breach and much larger illegal breaches in the official trade monopoly, the Spanish empire remained intact. English observers proclaimed it to be tottering on the verge of collapse, and English merchants would have liked their government to give it the final push; but in fact, under a new and more vigorous dynasty, Spanish America was to experience in the eighteenth century a thorough overhaul of administration, a considerable increase in territory, and a very great increase in trade and general prosperity.

Although on the winning side in the war, the Dutch on the whole were losers by the peace. They neither gained nor lost important territories, it is true; and in the East the work of securing their commercial supremacy by means of territorial dominion went on without interruption. But the long and desperate struggle with France overtaxed the strength of the United Provinces, and their naval and commercial power declined in relation to their neighbours. In concentrating upon the development of commercial shipping, the Dutch had always tended to neglect purely naval construction except in times of obvious emergency. After the close of the last war with England in 1674 the Dutch navy suffered severely from this neglect, for oak ships deteriorate very quickly unless rotten timbers are at once replaced; and the immense but highly specialised Dutch merchant marine was not easily adaptable to privateering war. At the same time, thanks to the energy and administrative ability of Colbert, the French navy had grown in size and efficiency, while French privateers prepared to enter upon a golden age. In the series of wars from 1688 to 1713, the task of holding the French at sea fell more and more to the English. When, towards the end of the seventeenth century, the French navy in its turn struck a period of neglect and decline, the chief beneficiaries were the English. The Dutch emerged from the wars seriously weakened economically and politically; and everywhere except in the East Indies their commercial and colonial initiative passed to England.

The losses of the French and Dutch were England's gain. After the capture of Gibraltar and the defeat of the French Toulon fleet off Malaga in 1704, the English navy was left supreme at sea; and despite French privateers, the volume of English commercial shipping increased yearly throughout the war. Clearances from English ports rose from 3,550 in 1710 to 5,807 in 1714. The peace treaty contained commercial concessions—the *Asiento* and the annual ship— which were certain to lead to trouble; but the mercantile interests of the day courted trouble. Hundreds of economic and political pamphlets and speeches urged an aggressive commercial and colonial policy upon the government. The pugnacious and overconfident tone of these speeches and writings betrayed a mood of exaggeration, almost of hysteria; but they were backed by real power. It is true that the English navy, like other navies, suffered from its periods of neglect, when the ships of the reserve fleet lay rotting at their moorings; and whenever war threatened, merchant seamen had to be hastily impressed to man the navy, while the Navigation Acts were suspended to allow foreigners to fill the empty berths in merchant ships. In spite of the moments of panic, however, English command of the sea was effectively challenged on relatively few occasions in the eighteenth century; and throughout most of the century it served a truculent and covetous imperialism. In all the vast areas disputed between England and France, territorial dominion naturally hung upon sea power; and a fleet cruising off Brest could defeat the purpose of the most formidable fortifications at Louisbourg or Pondicherry.

EPILOGUE: THE BOUNDS OF

CHRISTENDOM, 1715

By the beginning of the eighteenth century European merchants, missionaries and planters had founded permanent settlements in all the continents of the world except Australia and the Antarctic. The nature of these settlements varied greatly; but all alike depended upon a mother country in Europe. None was self-supporting; none yet aspired to independence of the founding state, though some colonies had changed hands as a result of European wars, and many were to change hands in the eighteenth century. In spite of this common dependence, there was a wide diversity between different types of colony. The hold of the European nations upon many of their outposts was still weak. Only a few relatively small areas could be said to be Europeanised, and the most potent factor in determining the nature of a European colony was the character of the native race among whom it was planted.

In some parts of the world Europeans had settled as a permanent resident aristocracy among more primitive, but settled peoples, living by their labour and to a varying extent inter-marrying with them. This was the situation in Spanish and Portuguese America; though the areas under effective European government still covered only a part of the immense regions claimed by Portugal and Spain, and no province was without its Indian 'frontier'. In the West Indies also, Europeans formed a resident aristocracy, though the primitive labour force there was not native but imported.

In other regions, where the native population was too sparse or too intractable to furnish an adequate labour force, and where Negroes could not thrive, Europeans had cleared the land, pushed the natives aside, and formed purely European communities, living largely by their own labour as farmers, fishermen or traders. A thin fringe of settlements of this type stretched along the Atlantic sea-board of North America; settlements with busy towns and har-bours looking towards Europe, but with a dangerous forest frontier not far inland. English and French America still lagged far behind Spanish America in population, wealth and cultural attainments, but was growing rapidly in strength and assertiveness.

In the Old World, Europeans had concentrated their efforts upon regions known to produce articles of value, and armed commercial monopoly rather than empire had been their principal object. In West Africa, source of slaves and ivory, the climate prevented them from settling. In most parts of the East they found civilised peoples, powerful and numerous enough to resist the settlement of Europeans as a resident aristocracy. Europeans had invaded the East as cru-saders, as armed traders and as pirates. By developing their technical advantages in shipping and armament, by exploiting oriental dis-sensions, by using force here and diplomacy there, they had secured commercial footholds in many parts of the East; but they were far from ruling as overlords. Except for a few small areas in Malabar and in the East Indian islands, their actual possessions were still confined to forts and trading factories.

With all these qualifications, the spectacle of European world-wide power was already impressive. It was long since the process of expansion had suffered a major set-back. Even the humiliation of the English East India Company at the hands of Aurangzeb had had but little permanent effect upon the fortunes of the English in India. The colonising peoples of western Europe looked out upon the world with eager and greedy confidence. Their vital technical superiority in ships and guns was increasing. The late seventeenth and early eighteenth centuries saw great improvements in the rig of sea-going ships, notably the introduction of fore-and-aft head-sails working on the stays and a little later the transformation of the cumbersome lateen mizen into the fore-and-aft 'spanker'. Both the art of navigation and the design of navigators' instruments were ad-vancing rapidly, with the increasing application of scientific know-ledge to technical development. The design of guns, it is true, was changing little; but guns were increasing in size, and the iron-found-ing industry which produced them was developing fast, especially in England. Throughout the eighteenth century the colonising nations expanded their trade, added to their territory and exported emigrants at an ever-increasing rate. As their acquisitions increased, their determination to dominate certain favoured areas increased also. In no other century in European history was there more constant and more bitter fighting over the possession of colonial territory. The fighting now took the form of full-scale war in Europe and at sea, as well as the familiar quarrels between rival colonising groups overseas. Disputes over colonial territory and trade had become too serious to lie outside the normal orbit of European diplomacy, as they had done to some extent in former centuries.

The aims and methods of territorial and commercial expansion had changed profoundly in three hundred years. In the East, the original object of European commercial intrusion had been to establish a monopolistic trade to Europe in small quantities of rare and valuable products, such as spices, silk and precious stones. The Portuguese had obtained these cargoes for themselves, and denied them to others, as often by force or threats of force as by peaceful trading. Their commerce was very close to piracy. By the early eighteenth century European traders in the East had developed in addition a much greater bulk of trade with Europe and between Eastern countries in commodities which were in high demand without being particularly valuable or rare: cotton cloth, rice and coffee. To maintain monopolies in all these commodities, it was necessary to control their production so as to ensure a steady but exclusive supply. From being a disturbing predatory element in Eastern commerce, the European trading companies were becoming settled powers, exacting tribute as well as monopolising trade, each interested in the maintenance of stable and profitable conditions in its own area. Each group was intensely jealous of other Europeans and was ready to exploit local disputes in order to protect or extend the sphere of its own operations.

In the New World the order of development was reversed. Conquest and settlement, not commerce, had been the objects almost from the start. Since resistance was relatively weak, stable European communities ruling considerable tracts of country, with or without native labour, emerged quickly from the initial stage of fighting and treasure-hunting. Once these communities were established, however, their trade with Europe became a vital consideration. By the early eighteenth century the attention of colonising governments was concentrated mainly upon territories which produced large quantities of exportable raw materials and which provided stable and exclusive markets for the products of their home countries. Colonial administration and colonial wars in the New World as in the Old were more and more coming to serve the ends of commerce to the exclusion of other considerations.

Buccaneering had ceased to be a semi-respectable profession; but the slave trade, which supplied the labour for sugar and tobacco plantations, was in its heyday. Slaves were wanted not only in Spanish and Portuguese America and in the West Indies, but increasingly in the plantations of Virginia, Carolina, Georgia and Louisiana. The eighteenth-century slave trade, with the warm approval of government, made the port of Liverpool and was an important factor in the commercial predominance of England.

Negro slaves were not the only unwilling emigrants to the New World. With the steady development of industry in England in the eighteenth century, 'colonies of settlement' came back into official favour as markets for manufactures, and government approval was assured for any effort made to populate them. In England there was no longer religious persecution or civil strife to drive people overseas; but in other parts of Europe, especially in Ireland and the Palatinate, recurrent famine and war were leaving thousands of families destitute. Labour was needed in the colonies at almost any price. The captains of trans-Atlantic packets used every method from persuasive advertisement to kidnapping to induce these unfortunates to emigrate. The seventeenth-century trickle of non-English emigrants to English America became in the early eighteenth century a steady stream. The long line of the Indian frontier, which had been more or less stationary in the later seventeenth century, began to roll steadily back towards the mountains in the early eighteenth.

In these 'colonies of settlement', where the natives were relatively few and primitive, European advance was not seriously retarded either by Indian resistance or by any great tenderness for Indian interests. But where the Indians were numerous and docile, the increasing concentration upon commercial objects accompanied and reflected a steady change in the attitude both of governments and of colonists towards native races. The old crusading spirit in which the expansion movement was conceived had disappeared in the course of the sixteenth century. The holy war against the infidel could appeal in full force only to peoples who had felt themselves seriously threatened by Islam. The plunder and devastation which accompanied the holy war could not be carried on indefinitely against peoples who submitted, however unwillingly, to European government. Conversion by the sword was repudiated in the sixteenth century both by theologians and by conscientious administrators.

In the colonies of the Catholic powers in the sixteenth century the period of crusading war and plunder had been succeeded by a period of deep and thoughtful missionary fervour. In Spanish America above all the Church had striven not only to convert but to teach the Indians, and to recruit and train an educated native priesthood. By the end of the sixteenth century, it is true, the Spanish missionaries' attitude towards the Christian Indian was becoming less optimistic. The ideal of a native priesthood was abandoned, partly through conviction of its hopelessness, partly through social opposition from secular sources. The principle upon which Las Casas had insisted so strongly, that the Indian was potentially the spiritual and intellectual equal of the European, was less emphatically urged in the seventeenth century both by theologians and by those who professed to know the Indian. Nevertheless, the work of spreading the Faith went on in hundreds of Franciscan and Jesuit missions, penetrating into remote regions of the Americas far beyond the limits of ordinary white settlement. In the Portuguese East also, the work of Jesuit missionaries went on steadily, though often discredited by the piracies which their countrymen committed. In Europe the establishment in 1622 of the Propaganda—the Congregation for the propagation of the Faith—evinced the direct concern of the Papacy in colonial missions, in the training of missionaries, and once again in the creation of native priesthoods.

In the late seventeenth century, despite the efforts of the Propaganda, missionary enterprise began to slacken. The growing weakness of Spanish and Portuguese colonial government and French preoccupation with European affairs together caused a loss of effective support. The general intellectual temper of Europe, also, grew less favourable to missions. In the eighteenth century, a rationalistic humanism, often antagonistic to Christianity, was to sap the religious enthusiasm of educated people throughout western Europe, and the decline of Catholic missionary effort was to be accentuated by the expulsion of the Jesuit order from the territories of France, Portugal and Spain. Moreover, the main initiative in expansion was passing from the Catholic to the Protestant nations of Europe; and though many Dutchmen and Englishmen had carried abroad religious convictions of a most uncompromising kind, they had shown considerably less skill and enthusiasm than their Catholic rivals in missionary enterprise. There were in New England some notable exceptions. Societies were formed quite early in the seventeenth century for evangelising the North American Indians, but their achievements were comparatively small. The Dutch Calvinists in the East, particularly in Ceylon, made some converts, but mainly from Catholic Christianity; they made little impression upon the vigorous Buddhism of Ceylon, or upon Islam elsewhere. In general it was not to be expected that commercial concerns should spend much money or thought upon missionary work.

The general decline in missionary enthusiasm by the early eighteenth century was accompanied by a corresponding decline in a sense of responsibility for the material well-being of subject races. In Spanish America the alienation of Indian land, which the Hapsburgs had tried to prevent, proceeded rapidly under the Bourbons; peonage—debt-slavery—became more and more frequent; and the Indians were increasingly subjected to a new form of *repartimiento* —the forced sale of unwanted manufactured goods by local officials. The far-reaching reforms which the Bourbons introduced in Spanish colonial government, unlike much of the legislation of former years, was inspired by a desire to rationalise administration and foster trade rather than by concern for Indian interests. In Brazil the damage done by gold- and slave-hunting *bandeiras* went unchecked by government, though not unreproved by missionaries. In most parts of English America the relations between colonial government and Indian tribes in time of peace were mainly concerned with trade and the purchase of land, by treaties whose clauses often contained a studied ambiguity. The Indians were never regarded as subjects, in any close sense, of the English Crown. In the East the Dutch East India Company was imposing a peaceful and relatively tolerant rule upon the limited territories which it governed directly, but at the cost of a systematic and ruthless subordination of all native economic activity to the trading needs of the company.

The idea, so prominent in present-day theories of colonisation, that subject races should be trained to govern themselves in European fashion, has never been entirely absent from European thought. Several Spanish writers in the sixteenth century hinted at such a policy, and determined efforts were made to introduce municipal government of the Spanish type into Indian towns. Such theories had been largely abandoned by the early eighteenth century, though they never quite disappeared. John Archdale advocated an extensive scheme of Indian education in Carolina. He believed 'that the hand of God was eminently seen in thinning the Indians to make way for the English' but that the survivors should be taught that the English 'were once as they were, but were reduced into a civilised state by a Noble and Heroick Nation'. Nothing came of such proposals. In Europe as a whole, neither legislation, writings nor speeches in the early eighteenth century showed much evidence of a feeling that the possession of colonies carried with it a duty towards their non-European inhabitants.

The imperialism of eighteenth-century Europe had many ugly characteristics. It was truculent, cynical and greedy. It combined self-satisfaction with an insensitiveness to the sufferings of other peoples, repugnant not only to the best thought of our time, but to

that of the sixteenth century also. Of course greed and brutality
had marked every stage of the expansion; but in the earlier days
there had been a great sense of wonder, a certain humility under-
lying the truculence, sometimes an anxious searching of conscience.
It is difficult to avoid the conclusion that the general European attitude towards non-Europeans had coarsened and hardened with successful expansion. Familiarity had bred contempt.

Successful expansion was to continue throughout the eighteenth
and nineteenth centuries. Despite the constant colonial wars of the
eighteenth century, despite the successful political revolt of many
European colonial communities, the extension of European
influence was continuous, and in time a new sense of responsibility
developed. In the East, European governments belatedly recognised
that trading corporations, left to themselves, could not be expected
to administer vast non-European territories either efficiently or
justly. In the West, the slave trade was swept away by a strong and
surprisingly sudden growth of humanitarian feeling. The nineteenth
century saw the development for the first time of widespread missionary enthusiasm among the Protestant peoples—enthusiasm
which was to take a highly practical turn in medical and educational
directions. The foundations of the revival had indeed been laid in
the apparently unpropitious years of the eighteenth century. The
English Society for the Propagation of the Gospel was founded in
1701, largely for work among Negro slaves. The influence of such
bodies in that age of rationalism was at first very small, but later in
the century the Moravian communities, English Methodism and
other revival movements helped to stir public opinion in many parts
of Europe. In more recent times missionary societies of all kinds
have played an increasingly important part, not only in education
and evangelisation overseas, but in teaching European peoples a
sense of responsibility towards weaker races.

In 'trusteeship' Europe has at present a theory and a policy of
colonial government to which all colonising states profess at least
a formal adherence. The early eighteenth century had no such common theory; but the ideas upon which 'trusteeship' is based are
not new. They are all to be found in sixteenth and seventeenth-century doctrines of natural law. No firmer insistence could be found
than that of the great jurist, Vitoria, lecturing at Salamanca in 1532:

'These people' (the American Indians) 'are not unintelligent, but
primitive ; they are incapable of maintaining a civilised State according to the requirements of humanity and law ; . . . their government,
therefore should be entrusted to people of intelligence and experience,
as though they were children. . . . But this interference must be for

their welfare and in their interests, not merely for the profit of the Spaniards; for otherwise the Spaniards would be placing their own souls in peril.'

It might be argued that Vitoria's distinction was unreal, the expression of a corporate European hypocrisy. The missionary and the honest administrators, however well-intentioned, may be insidious destroyers of the culture of subject peoples and unconscious agents of the greed of the conquerors. This fact did not escape the notice of some of the early Spanish writers; it is mentioned frequently by the great missionary anthropologist, Sahagún, and in many official reports from Spanish America. Nowadays it is a commonplace that the sudden introduction of European law, European habits and European technical devices among people to whom they are unfamiliar may have disastrous results. These misgivings are yet another expression of a sense of imperial responsibility, of a conscious desire among thoughtful Europeans to soften, since they cannot prevent, the impact of one culture upon another, and to offer the best, not the worst, of European civilisation to the rest of the world. Vitoria's distinction was a real one. No nation undertakes the labour and expense of colonial expansion without hope of profit; but throughout the whole story of European expansion there has been conflict between an imperialism interested only in profits and an imperialism which accepts duties also. The feeling of duty, of responsibility, was relatively weak in the eighteenth century, weaker than it had been in the sixteenth, weaker than it is today; but it was never entirely absent. It was the product of a continuous missionary tradition running back to the thirteenth century.

SUGGESTIONS FOR FURTHER READING

GENERAL

BAKER, J. N. L., *A History of Geographical Discovery and Exploration* (London, 1931)

DICKINSON, R. E. and HOWARTH, O. J. R., *The Making of Geography* (Oxford, 1933)

LATOURETTE, K. S., *History of the Expansion of Christianity* (5 vols.), vol. III (London, 1944)

PENROSE, B., *Travel and Discovery in the Renaissance* (Cambridge, Mass., 1955)

PARRY, J. H., *The Age of Reconnaissance* (London, 1963)

CHAPTER 1

CIPOLLA, C. M., *Guns, sails and empires* (New York, 1965)

CRONE, G. R., *Maps and Their Makers* (London, 1953)

SINGER, C., HOLMYARD, E. J., HALL, A. R. and WILLIAMS, T. I., eds., *A History of Technology*, vol. III (Oxford, 1957)

TAYLOR, E. G. R., *The Haven-finding Art; a History of Navigation from Odysseus to Captain Cook* (London, 1956)

VARENDE, J. de la (trans. SAVILL, M.), *Cherish the Sea* (London, 1955)

CHAPTER 2

BLAKE, J. W., *European Beginnings in West Africa* (London, 1937)

BOVILL, E. W., *The Golden Trade of the Moors* (London, 1958)

JAYNE, K. G., *Vasco da Gama and his Successors, 1460–1580* (London, 1910)

PRESTAGE, E., *The Portuguese Pioneers* (London, 1933)

WHITEWAY, R. S., *The Rise of Portuguese Power in India, 1497–1550* (London, 1952)

CHAPTER 3

BEAGLEHOLE, J. C., *The Exploration of the Pacific* (London, 1934)
JANE, C. (trans.), VIGNERAS, L. A. (ed.), *The Journal of Christopher Columbus* (London, 1960)
MORISON, S. E., *Admiral of the Ocean Sea* (New York, 1940)
PARRY, J. H. and SHERLOCK, P. M., *A Short History of the West Indies* (London, 1959)
POHL, F. J., *Amerigo Vespucci: Pilot Major* (New York, 1944)

CHAPTER 4

DÍAZ DEL CASTILLO, BERNAL (MAUDSLAY, A. P., trans. and ed.), *The True History of the Conquest of New Spain*, 4 vols. (London, 1908–12)
KIRKPATRICK, F. A., *The Spanish Conquistadores* (London, 1946)
MERRIMAN, R. B., *The Rise of the Spanish Empire in the Old World and the New*, 4 vols. (New York, 1918–34)
PARRY, J. H., *The Spanish Seaborne Empire* (London, 1966)

CHAPTER 5

BREBNER, J. B., *The Explorers of North America, 1492–1806* (London 1933)
INNIS, H. A., *The Cod Fisheries* (New Haven, 1940)
JENKINSON, A. (MORGAN, E. D. and COOTE, C. H., eds.), *Early Voyages and Travels to Russia and Persia*, 2 vols. (London, 1886)
WILLIAMSON, J. A., *The Age of Drake* (London, 1946)
Hawkins of Plymouth (London, 1949)
Maritime Enterprise, 1485–1558 (Oxford, 1913)

CHAPTER 6

FOSTER, W., *England's Quest for Eastern Trade* (London, 1933)
LINSCHOTEN, JAN HUYGHEN VAN (BURNELL, A. C. and TIELE, P. A., eds.), *The Voyage of Jan Huyghen van Linschoten to the East Indies*, 2 vols. (London, 1885)
ROWSE, A. L., *The Expansion of Elizabethan England* (London, 1955)
SCOTT, W. R., *The History of Joint-stock Companies to 1720*, 2 vols (London, 1910–12)
VLEKKE, B., *The Story of the Dutch East Indies* (Cambridge, Mass., 1945)

CHAPTER 7

ANDREWS, C. M., *The Colonial Period of American History*, 4 vols. (New Haven, 1934–38)
ANDREWS, M. P., *The Soul of a Nation* (New York, 1944)

BEER, G. L., *The Origins of the British Colonial System, 1578–1660* (New York, 1908)

WERTENBAKER, T. J., *The First Americans* (New York, 1927)

CHAPTER 8

BARBOUR, V., *Capitalism in Amsterdam in the Seventeenth Century* (Baltimore, 1950)

BOURNE, E. G., *The Voyages of Champlain*, 2 vols. (New York, 1922)

BOXER, C. R., *The Dutch in Brazil* (Oxford, 1957)

NEWTON, A. P., *The European Nations in the West Indies, 1493–1688* (London, 1933)

PARKMAN, F., *Pioneers of France in the New World* (various eds.)

WRONG, G. M., *The Rise and Fall of New France* (London, 1928)

CHAPTER 9

BEER, G. L., *The Old Colonial System*, 2 vols. (New York, 1933)

HARPER, L. A., *The English Navigation Laws* (New York, 1939)

HECKSHER, E. F. (SHAPIRO, M., trans.), *Mercantilism*, 2 vols. (London, 1934)

THORNTON, A. P., *West India Policy under the Restoration* (Oxford, 1956)

CHAPTER 10

BOXER, C. R., *The Dutch Seaborne Empire* (London, 1965)

HUNTER, W. W., *History of British India, 1500–1700*, 2 vols. (London, 1899–1900)

PANIKKAR, K. M., *Asia and Western Dominance* (London, 1953)

VLEKKE, B., *Nusantara, a History of the East Indian archipelago* (Cambridge, Mass., 1945)

CHAPTER 11

BOXER, C. R., *Salvador de Sá and the Struggle for Brazil and Angola* (London, 1952)

DAVIES, K. G., *The Royal African Company* (London, 1957)

PARES, R., *War and Trade in the West Indies, 1739–1763* (Oxford, 1936)

WYNDHAM, H. A., *The Atlantic and Slavery* (Oxford, 1935)

INDEX

ABYSSINIA, 27
Acadia, 105, 108
Aden, 36
Affonso, King of Portugal, 29
Akbar, 82
Albuquerque, Affonso d', 35–8, 85
Alexander VI, Pope, 45
Almagro, Diego de, 57
Amazons Company, 99
Amboina, 32, 88, 91, 136
Andros, Sir Edmund, 128
annual ship, 157
Antilla, 42
Antilles, 99
Arabs, 8, 14, 16–17, 21, 33, 35
Archangel, 71
Archdale, John, 167
Arguim, 28
asientos, 155–8
astrolabe, 19
astronomy, 16–17
Ataide, Luis de, 81
audiencias, 63
Aurangzeb, 145–7
Azores, 40–2
Aztecs, 56
Azurara, Gomes Eannes de, 10, 26–7, 28

BABUR, 81
back-staff, 19
baghlas, 21
Bahía, 115
Balboa, Blasco Núñez de, 49
Banda Islands, 32, 88, 136, 141
Bantam, 83, 90, 91, 134, 136–7, 141

Barbados, 99–101, 120–1, 129, 153
Barents, William, 72
Batavia, 91, 134–7, 139, 141
Board of Trade and Plantations, 129
Bombay, 145, 148
buccaneers, 113–14, 126
Buddhism, 166
bulls:
   Ea quæ (1506), 50
   Inter cætera (1493), 45
   Præcelsæ devotionis (1514), 50
Byzantine Empire, 8

CABOT, John, 46, 49, 68
Cabot, Sebastian, 49, 70
Cabral, Pero Alvárez, 34
Cadamosto, Alvise da, 28–9
Calcutta, 146, 148
Calicut, 33, 34, 85
Canada, 105–10, 116, 131–2, 159
Canaries, 40–1
Cantino, Alberto, 69
Canton, 37
Cao, Diogo, 30
Cape Agulhas, 30
Cape Bojador, 27–8
Cape Blanco, 28
Cape Breton Island, 159
Cape Cross, 30
Cape of Good Hope, 30–1, 138
Cape Verde Islands, 40–1
captains-donatory, 115
caravels, 21–3, 43
Carolina, 121
Cartier, Jacques, 107

castles, 20
Ceuta, 10–11, 26
Ceylon, 32, 91, 135
Champlain, Samuel de, 108
Chancellor, Richard, 71–2
Charles I, King of England, 103, 105–6,
    108–9, 144
Charnock, Job, 146
charter colonies, 122
Child, Sir Josiah, 117
Chile, 57
cloves, 32, 37
Code noir, 154
Coen, Jan Pieterszoon, 91, 134–5
coffee, 142
Colbert, Jean-Baptiste, 130–2, 148, 160
Columbus, Christopher, 19, 31, 42–6
compass, 18
Congo, 30
Connecticut, 104, 121, 128
consulado, 66
convoys, 65–6
corregidores, 61
Corte-Real, Gaspar and Miguel, 69
Cortés, Hernando, 55–7
Cosa, Juan de la, 47
Costa Rica, 46
Council of the Indies, 63
councils, executive, 121, 128
Covilhã, Pedro da, 34
Cromwell, Oliver, 118
cross-staff, 19
crown colonies, 99, 120–1, 127
Crusades, 9–10
Cuba, 54
Curaçao, 113

D'AILLY, Cardinal Pierre, 15
Davis, John, 173
declination tables, 17
Del Cano, Sebastian, 52
Diamper, synod of, 86
Dias, Bartolomeu, 30–1, 34
Diu, 35, 82
Drake, Sir Francis, 77–8

EAST INDIA COMPANY, Dutch, 89–91,
    134–43, 167
East India Company, English, 86, 89–92,
    143–8, 163
East India Company, French, 148
Ehinger, 151
Elmina, 30, 152
encomienda, 60–2

engagés, 111
Eratosthenes, 14

FISHERIES, 68–70, 105
Fitch, Ralph, 87
fluyt, 118
fore-and-aft rig, 117
Fra Mauro, 29
Frobisher, Martin, 73

GALLEYS, 20
Gambia, 28
Gama, Vasco da, 31, 34
Georgia, 121
Gilbert, Sir Humphrey, 69–70, 73
Goa, 36–8, 81, 85
Golconda, 144, 146
Guadeloupe, 110
Guiana, 93, 99
Guiana Company, 99
Guinea Company, French, 157
Gujerat, 82, 92
Gulf Stream, 49
gun-ports, 25
gunnery, 24–5

HARDWICKE, Lord Chancellor, 154
Hawkins, Sir John, 73–6
Henry of Portugal, Prince, 11, 26–9,
    39–41
Heyn, Piet, 112
Hispaniola, 44, 54, 157
Honduras, 46
Hormuz, 36
House of Trade, Spanish, 66
Houtman, Cornelis de, 88
Hudson, Henry, 73
Hudson (river), 70, 102, 105, 116
Hudson's Bay, 159
Hudson's Bay Company, 132, 159
Hudson's Strait, 73
Humayun, 82

IBN MAJID, 31
Imago Mundi, 15
Incas, 56
indented servants, 97, 100
intendants, 130
Islam, 8–10, 33, 143, 166

JAMAICA, 153
James I, King of England, 93, 95–6, 98–9
James II, King of England, 127, 128
Janszoon, Willem, 138
Jenkins' ear, war of, 158
Jesuits, 85, 109, 115, 131, 166
John II, King of Portugal, 17, 30, 44

KANUA, battle of, 81
Krishna Raya, 80–1

LA SALLE, René-Robert, 131
Las Casas, Fray Bartolomé de, 59
lateen rig, 21–3
latitude, 16–18
le Clerc, François, 77
Leo X, Pope, 50
Linschoten, Jan Huyghan van, 87–8
log, 18
longitude, 18
Louisbourg, 159
Louisiana, 131, 159

MACASSAR, 136
Madeira, 40–1
Madras, 144–5, 148
Magellan, Ferdinand, 50
Majapahit, 83
Malabar, 33
Malacca, 33, 37, 91, 135
Marathas, 145, 146
Martinique, 110
Massachusetts, 94, 105, 120–2, 127–8
Massachusetts Bay Company, 104
Masulipatam, 144
Mataram, 83, 136–7, 141
Mayas, 56
Mendoza, Antonio de, 57
Menéndez de Avilés, Pedro, 75, 77
mestizos, 61
Mexico, 55–6
missions, 8, 61, 109, 166–9
Mississippi, 131
Moluccas, 32, 52, 83, 135
Morgan, Henry, 114
Morton, Thomas, 103
Mossel Bay, 31
Mughal Empire, 81–2, 92, 143–6
Muscovy Company, 72

nau, 21
navigation, 16–19

Navigation Acts, 118, 124–5, 152
Nestorians, 38, 85–6
New Amsterdam (New York), 116, 119, 127–8
New England, 96, 102–5, 120, 126–8
Newfoundland, 68, 69, 105, 159
New Haven, 104
New Netherland, 116–19, 127
New Orleans, 159
New Plymouth, 102
New Zealand, 138
Nova Scotia, 105, 158

PANIPAT, battle of, 81
Pennsylvania, 121
Peru, 56, 63
Philippines, 52, 57, 83
pirates, 126
Pizarro, Francisco, 56–7
Pizarro, Gonzalo, 58
Plantations Duties Act, 124–5
Po, Fernando, 29
Polo, Marco, 34
Pondicherry, 148
portolani, 15–16
Prester, John, 27
Propaganda, 166
proprietary colonies, 121, 127
Providence Company, 101
Ptolemy, 14
Pulicat, 144

QUADRANT, 19
Quebec, 105, 108

RALEIGH, Sir Walter, 93
Redemption Treaty, 117
regents, 140
repartimiento, 60, 62, 167
residents, 140
Rhode Island, 104
Ribault, Jean, 77
Richelieu, 108–10
Roe, Sir Thomas, 76, 92
Royal Africa Company, 153–4
Russia, 71–2

SAHAGÚN, Fray Bernadino de, 169
St Domingue, 159
St Kitts, 99, 110, 159

San Juan de Ulúa, battle of, 75
seigneuries, 109, 131
Sepúlveda, Juan Ginés de, 59
Seville, 66
Sierra Leone, 29
silver, 64-6
Sivaji, 145
slaves, 27-8, 54, 64-5, 74, 100-1, 114
slave trade, 74-6, 101, 150-8, 164-5
Smith, John, 98
Society for the propagation of the
    Gospel, 168
Socotra, 36
Solís, Juan Díaz de, 49, 51
Sound dues, 117
South Sea Company, 157-8
Spanish succession, war of, 158
Speelman, Cornelius, 136
spices, 32-7
square rig, 20, 23
Staple Act, 124-5
sugar, 40-1, 64, 74, 100-1, 111-12,
    114-16, 151-5
Sunda Strait, 135
Surat, 92, 143-5
Surinam, 112
Swally Roads, 92

Talikot, battle of, 81
Tasman, Abel, 138
Tasmania, 138
Ternate, 32, 83, 88, 136
Terra Australis Incognita, 138
Tidore, 32, 52, 135
timber, 40, 69, 96, 105, 117
Timur, 9
tobacco, 64, 98, 99, 100, 105, 111, 123-4
Toledo, Francisco de, 63
town-councils, 61, 104, 122
Tranquebar, 148

transportation, 97
Treaty of Alcaçovas (1479), 29
Treaty of Câteau-Cambrésis (1559), 76
Treaty of London (1604), 93
Treaty of Madrid (1670), 113
Treaty of Ryswyck (1697), 157
Treaty of St Germain-en-Laye (1632),
    105
Treaty of Saragossa (1529), 53
Treaty of Tordesillas (1494), 45, 50
Treaty of Utrecht (1713), 158-9
Trinidad, 45
tumble-home, 25
Turks, 8

Van Diemen, Anthony, 135
Vaughan, William, 95
Venice, 9
Vera Cruz, 56
Vespucci, Amérigo, 47-9
viceroys, 63
Vijayanagar, 33, 80-1
Virginia, 93, 94-5, 96-9, 120, 129
Virginia Company, 97
Vitoria, Francisco de, 168-9

West India Company, Dutch,
    111-13, 116-19
William III, King of England, 128
Willoughby, Sir Hugh, 71

Xavier, St Francis, 85

Zacuto, Abraham, 17